D1649121

**Denton Business Community
Prayer Breakfast**
dentonprayerbreakfast.org

Praise for Dee Ann Turner and It's My Pleasure

Dee Ann Turner publicly reveals, for the first time, the core DNA of Chick-fil-A's people selection process, which is the fundamental reason we are recognized among the top-ten brands in customer service, across all industries.

—Dan Cathy
Chairman, President and CEO, Chick-fil-A

Now there is an excellent response when people ask, "Why are customers so fanatically loyal to Chick-fil-A?" Go to someone who knows and take a look from an insider's viewpoint; read Dee Ann Turner's book *It's My Pleasure.*

—Jimmy Collins
Former President/COO, Chick-fil-A, Inc.
Author of *Creative Followership: In the Shadow of Greatness*

This is one of those rare books that contains such deceptively simple wisdom that you'll wonder, "Why doesn't every company do this?"

—Patrick Lencioni
President, The Table Group
Author of *The Five Dysfunctions of a Team* and *The Advantage*

Chick-fil-A is an extraordinary organization with one of the most distinctive and most powerful cultures I have ever studied. Dee Ann Turner has done a masterful job of allowing us to see into this culture and understand what makes it so vibrant and so strong.

—Marcus Buckingham
Founder, The Marcus Buckingham Company
Author of *StandOut* and Co-Author of *Now, Discover Your Strengths*

I love Chick-fil-A! The culture is a model for how to create great results for your people and your guests. Read Dee Ann Turner's *It's My Pleasure* and get your organization headed in the right direction.

—Ken Blanchard
Chief Spiritual Officer, The Ken Blanchard Companies
Co-Author of *The One Minute Manager* and
Leading at a Higher Level

The Chick-fil-A culture is one that inspires above and beyond performance in all they do to serve their customers. The company's model of excellence begins with their team and Dee Ann Turner's leadership has been an integral part of its success.

—**Paul Bowers**
Chairman, President and Chief Executive Officer
of Georgia Power

Every business owner, every leader, and every future leader who wants to lead well and create a thriving culture must read this book. *It's My Pleasure* is a thoughtful blueprint of how to build and sustain a healthy culture. Filled with timeless principles, engaging stories, and wise counsel, Dee Ann Turner has created the must-have book for leaders.

—**Alli Worthington**
COO of Propel Women
Author of *Breaking Busy*

Many people love and admire Chick-fil-A. This is a closer look at 'why.' Enjoy and be enriched!

—**Dr. Henry Cloud**
Author of *Boundaries: When to Say Yes,
How to Say No to Take Control of Your Life*

Creating and sustaining the right culture is a significant challenge for organizations. Dee Ann Turner is an engaging storyteller who offers practical wisdom on how leaders can create their own winning cultures by using the systems and principles used by Chick-fil-A. Turner's book is a great read that I highly recommend and plan to implement into the business and leadership curriculum at our university.

—**Dr. Kathryn Crockett,**
Program Coordinator MS in Leadership
Professor of Management and Leadership
Lubbock Christian University

In her book *It's My Pleasure*, Dee Ann Turner reminds us that people decisions are the most important ones you make. She believes that "who you take along on your journey" will determine your success. Complimentary cultures rooted in similar organizational values have been the hallmark of our successful partnership for nearly 15 years. It has been "Our Pleasure" to partner with Chick-fil-A to provide high-quality childcare for 350 children at their corporate campus. I can't think of a better example of their commitment to caring for their employees personally than to care for their employees' children.

—Mary Ann Tocio,
President and Chief Operating Officer, Bright Horizons

Dee Ann Turner takes us inside of Chick-fil-A's culture and introduces us to a company that cultivates the talents and dreams of its people. This is an inspiring read about the intentionality of investing in excellence. Chick-fil-A seeks to demonstrate integrity, generosity, and loyalty at all levels of leadership and customer service.

—Gary Haugen
President of International Justice Mission
Author of *The Locust Effect*

Every organization has its own unique culture and Chick-fil-A is no different. Dee Ann Turner has described the experiences and foundational elements that drive the success of Chick-fil-A and shape this culture. While your work environment may be different, there are nuggets of learning for everyone.

—Coretha Rushing
SVP, Chief Human Resource Officer. Equifax, Inc.
former EVP, Chief Human Resources Officer,
The Coca-Cola Company

It's My Pleasure is wonderful. It's easy-to-read, conversational tone is written with clear purpose, and it is filled with stories that illustrate each guiding principle. As an HR leader, I welcome Turner's thoughts on how best to build a much-admired organization, beginning with hiring for character, competency and chemistry. HR leaders take note—this is a book to read and to share with your staff. You'll be glad you did!

—Nancy Vepraskas
SVP of HR, United Way of Greater Atlanta,
President of P2Excellence.

Chick-fil-A has set the standard for the ultimate in customer service, and its success has shown the results. How it was accomplished is told in this book in a way that businesses of all types can benefit from. Wonderful, inspiring, and well written; I thoroughly enjoyed reading it.

—Kenneth H. Cooper, MD, MPH
Founder and Chairman,
Cooper Aerobics

Dee Ann Turner is authentic, compelling, and insightful. Whether for business or personal relationships, *It's My Pleasure* is a must-read book for anyone who wants to succeed.

—Kathrine Lee
Life and Business Strategist,
Founder of the Pure Hope Foundation

Dee Ann's fascinating book describes in wonderful detail the development of Chick-fil-A's culture, and why it became a cornerstone for its success. I loved reading Dee Ann's book because I knew she was a key builder and sustainer of the culture. I highly recommend *It's My Pleasure* for those who want to learn why corporate success is based on an 'inside/out' formula."

—Robert R. Buck
Chairman, Beacon Roofing Supply
Author of *Well Built*

IT'S
MY
PLEASURE

IT'S
MY
PLEASURE

THE IMPACT OF
EXTRAORDINARY TALENT
AND A COMPELLING CULTURE

DEE ANN TURNER

VICE PRESIDENT, CORPORATE TALENT, CHICK-FIL-A

elevate

For permission requests, please address Elevate Publishing

Editorial Content: AnnaMarie McHargue
Cover Design: Arthur Cherry

This book may be purchased in bulk for educational, business, organizational or promotional use.
For more information, please email info@elevatepub.com.

Published by Elevate, a division of Elevate Publishing, Boise, ID
ISBN-13: 978-1937498887

Printed in China

Library of Congress Control Number: 2015945897

Proceeds from the sale of this book will benefit domestic and global initiatives that support women, children and youth education.

Those who drink the water cannot forget
the one who dug the well.
Ancient Chinese Proverb

In memory of
The well digger, S. Truett Cathy, the author of
the phenomenal culture that is Chick-fil-A

For Andrew T. Cathy
May the future be immeasurably more
than you hope or imagine

CONTENTS

FOREWORD

In the 1980s and 1990s, Jack Welch used a forthright management style to cultivate a global mystique at GE's Crotonville campus. By the turn of the century, Welch was the most celebrated CEO in the world and General Electric was a brand known for its premier leadership. GE leaders were among the most sought after talent across any industry, and companies from every country began looking for ways to model what they were doing.

While we haven't taken quite the same approach to growth and talent development over our 68-year history, we have strived for it to be said of Chick-fil-A that our talent is the best in the industry, and that our "small-company," family culture is amazing to observe. In that way, we aspire to be the GE of our generation. I believe this book will make it clear why and how we go about it.

In the following pages, Dee Ann publicly reveals for the first time the core DNA of Chick-fil-A's people selection process, which is the fundamental reason we are recognized among the top ten brands in customer service, across all industries. Our unique talent selection and leadership development systems have also contributed to Chick-fil-A becoming the top selling quick-service chicken chain in the U.S., surpassing our nearest competitor by generating twice the average restaurant sales despite operating one less day (Sunday) per week.

When my dad, Truett Cathy, laid the foundation for the company nearly 70 years ago, he made it clear that the work was all about putting people first. When Jimmy Collins, the company's first president joined Chick-fil-A, he began to construct the systems that would help us continue to make great people decisions. And for the better part of three decades, it has been Dee Ann's job to ensure that we adhere to these same principles for not only selecting great talent, but training and retaining talented people throughout their careers.

Through previously untold stories shared in a warm and engaging style, this book reveals that the secret sauce of Chick-fil-A is not on the chicken; it's in the clarification and deliberate transfer of timeless principles from one generation of leaders to the next. Dee Ann does a remarkable job of not only describing these principles but also illustrating how they are communicated and lived out daily by our remarkable people.

These principles are not simply nice ideas. They are road-tested over seven decades involving tens of thousands of individuals. And it all starts with selecting great people. From the earliest days, my dad believed that if we selected the right people to operate the restaurants and then stewarded their talent well, all the other problems would be solved. He was right. Chick-fil-A franchisees continue to do a phenomenal job of selecting and leading top talent for their restaurants, which shows above all else in the way their team members serve guests every day.

We know that when we select great people, the performance of the restaurants increases. This creates more opportunities for Chick-fil-A franchisees, their teams, and staff members at the home office, which creates a higher demand to be a part of our company. This increased demand creates a larger pool of talented people to choose from, which allows us to be even more selective with the talent we choose. With this steady uptick in talent comes a steady uptick in performance at our restaurants and the home office. This creates even more opportunities which in turn attracts even greater talent. And thus the flywheel begins spinning.

Our talent selection and leadership development systems are a key reason we attract over 25,000 annual applicants for our corporate office, and over 30,000 annual applicants to become Chick-fil-A restaurant franchisees. It is also why the majority of our corporate staff members and many franchisees remain with the company their entire career. The selection and fulfillment of their talent is central to the sales growth we've been blessed with for more than 30 years in a row.

If anyone has ever wondered what draws so many people to Chick-fil-A, and what makes the culture so unique, this book will definitively answer the questions. I believe it will also become a classic inside and outside company walls. I am already looking forward to reading it for a second time.

Dan T. Cathy

INTRODUCTION
DESTINY IS A FUNNY THING

Some memories are imprinted on our minds forever, and the feelings they elicit are stamped on our hearts. At Disney, they say it all began with a mouse. For me, at Chick-fil-A, it all began with a flat tire.

When I began pursuing a job at Chick-fil-A, I knew very little about the company. I grew up in Atlanta eating at Chick-fil-A every time we went to the mall and fell in love with the sandwich right from the start. My husband and I had our first date there when I was still in high school, and my mother and I had lunch at Chick-fil-A on my wedding day.

Soon after we were married, my husband was hired to be the pastor at a church down the road from the Chick-fil-A Corporate office. Several young people in the youth group worked in the warehouse at Chick-fil-A and invited him to lunch at the office. Each time he went, he would tell me about the beautiful campus, the friendly people and the incredible culture. He soon began encouraging me to apply for a job at Chick-fil-A.

After some coaxing, I finally did apply for a job in Marketing, since I was currently working in the advertising field. I filled out the twelve-page application and mailed it in to Human Resources. Two weeks later, I received my first rejection letter and I thought, "Well, that is that." Not as easily deterred, my husband continued to encourage me to follow up and apply again. I did and received a second rejection letter. By this time, I was becoming intrigued and had learned enough about Chick-fil-A to know that I was very interested, but not sure how I was going to even get an interview, much less be hired.

After about six months of follow-up phone calls, I was about ready to give up on the idea. One day, a woman came into the church and explained to my husband that she had a flat tire and needed to call for help. Instead, he gladly changed the tire for her. When he finished, she gave him a coupon (known as a *Be Our Guest* card) for a free Chick-fil-A sandwich®. He quickly unearthed that she was an employee with Chick-fil-A, but had to resign because her husband was being relocated out of state. He asked her what department she worked in and she replied, "Advertising."

As soon as the woman left the church, my zealous husband quickly called me and informed me that Chick-fil-A had an opening in the advertising department—my specialty. I just as quickly picked up the phone and called the same sweet voice in Human Resources for the "umpteenth" time. I guess at this point, they decided I was not going away easily, and I was invited to come in to interview for the job.

Similar to the three follow-up interviews I would have later, my first interview was an all-day visit. I met with members of the Human Resources staff and various members of the Marketing department. The longer I sat on the sofa in the reception area, the more my desire to work for Chick-fil-A grew. I was amazed at the friendliness of the people, especially as I compared it to the firm where I currently worked. What a stark contrast! As I waited for the next interview, the same kind receptionist who had answered all of my many phone calls offered me coffee, soft drinks and juices from the break room, all provided at no cost to employees and guests. We dined in the company cafe where a gourmet lunch is provided to employees and guests. I toured the fitness center, complete with full-sized racquetball court, and I reviewed the exhaustive list of benefits, including the opportunity to reserve one of Truett Cathy's Florida beach condos for a week—a gift he provided to staff and others at that time.

Then came what was perhaps the most meaningful moment to me. As I sat on the sofa in the reception area, I had the opportunity to meet members of the Cathy family and other company leaders as they exited the elevator on the fifth floor. On my second visit, I sat waiting when a gentleman walked up and introduced himself. "I am Truett Cathy. Thank you for visiting today." Thirty years later, we still try to communicate that same level of personal care to our candidates as we get to know one another.

Eventually, after about four months of interviewing, checking references and skill testing, I made it to my final interview. Along the way, I also had been given the opportunity to consider a position within Human Resources. It was a tough decision between the two roles and the two departments; I had no idea at the time that this choice would determine the course of my career for decades. Advertising was truly my first love, but I was curious about a different role and a change of pace. My plan was to begin my career in Human Resources and make a move to Marketing within a couple of years. Obviously, that move has not yet occurred, even thirty years later.

This final interview was with Jimmy Collins, who, at the time, was Executive Vice President. Only recently had Jimmy taken over from Truett the responsibility of final hiring interviews. Because Truett believed that decisions about people were the most important decisions, he made sure he was included in the selection process for both staff and restaurant Operators. Once Jimmy received these new responsibilities, the interviews continued to be challenging! He also took great care with those decisions and noticed every detail. He was thoughtful and intense; he was also observant. Were the applicant's shoes new or shined? Did the candidate wear a watch? Were all the statements in the application true? To Jimmy, new shoes or polished old ones made a statement about professionalism and how much the candidate cared about getting the job. A watch indicated someone who was aware of time, had places to go and made promptness a habit. He was a fact checker on the application. Any slight embellishment or untruth indicated an integrity issue. I remember the question that he asked me that caused me to pause and wonder if I would not get the job: "Are you a perfectionist?" I responded that I believed that I was. He said, "Are the shoes in your closet in order?" When he asked that question, I knew that I was not a *true* perfectionist!

Jimmy ended my interview by telling me it was his responsibility to talk me out of the job. I was completely surprised. Why would a potential employer try to talk a candidate out of the job? He told me much of Chick-fil-A's success was based on long-term relationships . . . and employment was one of those long-term relationships. He said that if I could be talked out of this decision today, it would be better than in six months or a year when I chose to resign my job, impact my family and make other changes. To this day, I continue to have this conversation with every candidate. It's an important question. Of course, at the time, in my youth, I was thinking to myself, *Are you kidding me? After this four-month interviewing process and hours sitting on the reception sofa, I am absolutely sure I want this job.* Actually, that is almost verbatim what I said to Jimmy.

Late in the day on an October evening, I returned to the vice president's office (which is actually my office now) and accepted the lateral offer to leave my company and join Chick-fil-A. I thought it would be a wonderful place to work for a few years until we decided to start our family. Then, I would stay home with my children and be the pastor's wife. Destiny is a funny thing.

That night, I stood at the railing of the atrium, the very place I often stand today, to reflect on the five floors below and the career I saw ahead of me. I can still re-create the excitement that I had inside of me that night I was hired. I knew I had just become a part of something truly special. There was no possible way at such a young age and so inexperienced at life that I could, in any way, imagine the opportunities that were about to come my way. However, that was the beginning of a journey that shaped my entire adult life. The relationships, business knowledge, experiences and life lessons to follow have been nothing short of remarkable. And to think—it all started with a flat tire.

THE ESSENCE OF A
COMPELLING CULTURE

The culture of an institution, I've come to learn, is not just one of the things you manage. It ultimately affects everything that goes on in the institution. You have to understand it, shape it, and talk about it, and you have to lead it.

—Lou Gerstner, CEO, IBM (retired)

Ray had just finished the night shift on the assembly line at the local auto plant before grabbing a stool at the counter of his favorite restaurant. Within moments after sitting down, his usual order was placed in front of him. Just as he was pouring sugar in his hot coffee, Marie walked over with a big smile and a hearty "Good morning, Ray!" Ray came in every morning, sat on the same stool and ate the same "two eggs over easy, bacon, grits, toast and coffee." At this restaurant, they knew more than his usual order; they knew his name and his story. The employees were like family to him. Still a few years from retirement, Ray worked 8-hour shifts and sometimes overtime if it was available. His wife had died suddenly a few years before and their three grown children lived out of town.

Sometimes, when Ray was feeling lonely, he wandered into the restaurant, not just for the 15-cent cup of coffee, but for the smiles and warm greetings he was sure to receive. Most of the time, the owner was there visiting with customers and serving kindness right along with the meals. This was long before the restaurant would be Home to the Original Chicken Sandwich® and before the launch of a multi-billion dollar chain that birthed thousands of restaurants. It was before a single employee had spoken the signature "my pleasure," and long before anyone thought to promote the marketing strategies that offered second-mile service and emotional connections with customers. But all of those elements were already in place, because Truett Cathy led that way.

Truett modeled servant leadership before it had a name or was all the rage among business gurus. From the very beginning, he based his business on Biblical principles and that made it clear how he would treat his employees and his guests. When society changed, Truett did not, and it made all the difference for his business and his influence.

Truett believed that businesses are built on growing relationships with customers. Culture is created by the stories those relationships tell. Like Ray's story, every story contributes to the shaping of an organization, and each guest and team member does not just have a story; they *are* a story. Understanding each other this way unites our individual differences, maximizes our strengths and helps us to create a remarkable culture together.

For nearly 30 years until his passing in 2014, I had the opportunity to witness Truett Cathy firsthand as he worked to build a small, regional restaurant company into the number-one chicken restaurant chain in America. More importantly, I learned from him the importance of selecting and growing great talent and coaching that talent to preserve and strengthen a phenomenal culture. Truett always believed that if you select the right person again and again, that the collection of the character, competency and chemistry of those people would develop and strengthen the culture over time.

For Truett, it was always about the person—the guest, the team member, the Operator, the staff member—one person at a time. He often said, "We are not in the chicken business. We are in the people business." As a human resources professional, how could I not be attracted to such a philosophy? In fact, it was that spirit that encouraged me to remain at Chick-fil-A for what has now been more than 30 years.

In some ways, by following in the footsteps of my predecessors, a small part of Chick-fil-A's culture was cultivated in my office, where I was able to experience the greatest joy and reward of my career: hearing the stories of people's lives. In my office, where candidates nervously sat on my little red couch (that later was re-covered blue), I learned their backgrounds, interests and dreams. It was an honor to be a "facilitator of opportunity" on behalf of Truett Cathy. For not only was I working on behalf of Truett Cathy to strengthen the brand through the selection of Operators and staff, I personally reaped the benefits of his words and was transformed by his influence. His integrity caused me to examine my character to reflect integrity. His loyalty to guests, Operators, staff, vendors, and friends called me to a life of loyalty to Chick-fil-A and its people. His generosity influenced me to give of my time, talent and treasure to others. And, his commitment to excellence inspired me to do my best and give my best every day in every way. His example provided us with just the right words to describe our core values at Chick-fil-A: integrity, loyalty, generosity and excellence.

It has been my pleasure to serve Truett and Chick-fil-A and to watch the dreams of others be fulfilled and multiplied. In return, Chick-fil-A has enjoyed the rewards of its commitment to attracting extraordinary talent, cultivating a compelling culture and creating enduring impact.

ONE

CREATING A
COMPELLING CULTURE

Creating a strong, compelling culture requires intentionality and vision. This creation cannot happen instantly or accidentally. A visionary must imagine the future and then design the path to align the organization with that future.

Culture is the soul of the organization. It is the way we envision, engage and experience others within an organization. Culture defines the values and behaviors that are acceptable and expected. Culture can be an elusive concept to describe, but at Chick-fil-A, we call it living life together. It is far easier to create a compelling culture from the beginning than to rebrand a struggling culture later, so it's an essential beginning, not just to a business, but also to any organization—regardless of the type of business.

To build a compelling culture, your organization must take several critical steps.

A compelling culture begins with **a clear purpose for existing**. In other words: WHY are we in business? If culture is the soul of the organization, then the purpose is the heart of it, for what unites an organization is a common purpose, a reason for existence. For our business, we have a higher calling than just selling chicken. From early on, our company ownership decided that stewardship and influence were key motivators. Sure, serving great food in a clean environment by friendly and courteous people is what we do. But selling chicken is a means to glorify God by being faithful stewards and having a positive influence. That is our purpose.

Ideally, an organization might establish its purpose early, but sometimes internal or external factors cause the organization to either establish a purpose or rewrite its original one. Chick-fil-A did not establish its well-known corporate purpose until 1982, nearly 20 years after its incorporation. Facing an uncertain economy, a first-ever slump in sales and debt incurred by the opening of a new corporate campus, Truett had to rally the troops. He met with Chick-fil-A's executive committee to contemplate what to do about their current challenges. When they finished their discussion, they had not decided on a new marketing plan to boost sales, nor did they establish a cost reduction plan to better manage the debt. They instead emerged with a well-defined purpose for being in business at all: "To glorify God by being a faithful steward of all that has been entrusted to us. To be a positive influence on all who come in contact with Chick-fil-A." This Corporate Purpose was carved into a stone pedestal and now sits at the front door to our corporate headquarters in Atlanta. It serves as a daily reminder to everyone who passes through our doors what we are in business to do.

Truett and his leaders realized that to motivate our staff to serve Chick-fil-A Operators and to motivate Operators to grow their businesses over time; we had to be about more than just selling chicken. Selling chicken is a means to a much more significant end. So what were the results of creating a meaningful purpose and carving it in stone? Chick-fil-A has experienced phenomenal sales growth every year since 1983 and in 2012, the company became debt-free. Knowing why we truly exist helps us succeed at everything we do.

The next step to growing a compelling culture is **a challenging mission**. WHAT are we in business to do? Over time a mission might change depending on the goals of the organization, so it should be evaluated continually. For example, the Orlando Magic's mission statement is: "To be world champions on and off the court, delivering legendary moments every step of the way." The organization clearly aspires to be world basketball champions and to deliver special experiences for their fans both on and off the court.

Determining core values is the next crucial decision necessary to create a compelling culture. These values are the fundamental beliefs that inform decisions, actions and behaviors and rest at the heart of the culture. Core values answer these key questions: What do we believe in? Do we have experiences in our organization that support our beliefs? HOW do we express those beliefs? To identify core values is to select a few of the very most important attributes that our teams and organizations can remember and live out day-to-day. Teach for America has five core values that describe the behavior expected to fulfill their mission, which is to "grow leaders who work to ensure that kids growing up in poverty get an excellent education." Their five core values of transformational change, leadership, team, diversity and respect and humility are critical to achieving their mission. When the core values of an organization match the purpose and the mission, they inspire that organization's members to play an integral role in the organization's success.

Chick-fil-A's core values were chosen from the model Truett provided. He exemplified many commendable traits, but, to our organization, four stood out above all others: Excellence, Integrity, Generosity and Loyalty.

> **Businesses do not become excellent in the big areas without focusing on the small details, too.**

Excellence in product and service is the backbone of success for any business. However, businesses do not become excellent in the big areas without focusing on the small details, too. For years, former Chick-fil-A President and COO Jimmy Collins reviewed all company communication. As part of our culture, it was unacceptable to send communication with errors in it, and Jimmy made sure that Chick-fil-A's internal and external communication reflected excellence. Our offices are meticulously clean and orderly, and the expectation is that a guest will find the back of the house at a Chick-fil-A restaurant clean and orderly, too. Jimmy was known for stopping his car on the busy exit ramp leading to the Chick-fil-A Corporate office to pick up trash along the roadway. Even though that roadway is the responsibility of the local municipality, they did not keep the exit ramp clear of trash, so Jimmy did it for them. To this day, our own staff cleans that exit ramp because we want guests to have a remarkable experience from the moment they exit the highway and head toward Chick-fil-A. Excellence in small things leads to excellence in big things.

Integrity was another core value constantly demonstrated by Truett. At the heart of integrity is trust. Guests, Operators, team members and staff all have to trust that we will do what we say we will do, how we say we will do it, and when we say we will do it. The food not only has to be excellent and safe, but it also should taste the same whether served in California or Washington, D.C.

The greatest example of Truett's integrity was his decision to remain closed on Sundays. He believed that everyone needed a day each week to rest and focus on family or other interests. That policy has been extremely beneficial to team members who enjoy being assured of a consistent day off. Early in Chick-fil-A's growth, this commitment prevented Chick-fil-A from entering into several prime mall locations. Regardless of the sales growth this would have created for Chick-fil-A through more rapid expansion, Truett held firm to his decision. In the end, what the mall landlords learned is that Chick-fil-A produced as much sales in six days as the other food tenants did in seven. In almost every case, Chick-fil-A had the highest volume of sales out of all the food tenants in the mall. Eventually, Chick-fil-A became a sought-after tenant in major and regional malls and later as a freestanding or inline tenant.

> Truett was often asked if he had calculated how much sales he lost by being closed on Sunday. He always responded that he was more concerned with how much sales he would have lost had he remained open.

Truett was often asked if he had calculated how much sales he lost by being closed on Sunday. He always responded that he was more concerned with how much sales he would have lost had he remained open. To this day, all Chick-fil-A restaurants are closed on Sunday. It is a commitment that Truett's children have promised to continue and a testament to the lasting value of integrity.

Generosity was at the heart of who Truett was, so much so that he wrote a book entitled *The Generosity Factor*. Truett believed in the principle of tithing. In any given year, a portion of Chick-fil-A's income is given away, including to Chick-fil-A's own foundation, The Chick-fil-A Foundation, which supports youth and educational programs. Personally, Truett tithed in times of less and plenty. The principle of stewardship was very important to Truett because it brought him great joy to be generous. He knew if he was a good steward of his resources that he would have more opportunity to do what he loved—give to others. The Operator model itself is a testimony to Truett's generosity. Through it, he gave thousands of people the opportunity to operate their own business.

Indeed, Truett's generosity was a model for the entire Chick-fil-A organization and many have followed in his footsteps, serving and giving to non-profit organizations and those in need all over the world. One of the ways Chick-fil-A uses resources to impact both the organization and other people is through international service trips where Operators and staff teach leadership skills. One such team made a significant impact on a young man in Mexico. This team of Operators presented Chick-fil-A's leadership model, the SERVE Model©, to a group of young entrepreneurs in Mexico City. At Chick-fil-A, leaders SERVE, which means they do five things: See and shape the future; Engage and develop others; Reinvent continuously; Value results and relationships and Embody the company values. During this session in Mexico, there was time for Q&A. This young man eagerly jumped up to share his dream. He was a chef planning to open a restaurant and the SERVE Model© intrigued him. Although the odds were stacked against him, he was determined to use his chef skills to find him opportunities in the restaurant business. After the presentation, he gave each of the Operators attending his business card, along with a jar of salad dressing that he had created.

Four years later, two of the Operators from that trip returned to Mexico City to volunteer at a different organization. They were meeting in a private home and enjoying a catered meal. When the two Operators reached the meat carving station, a gentleman asked if they remembered him. It was the young chef that they had met four years earlier. He thanked the two Operators and explained how the training they had provided had changed his life. He now owns three restaurants and has twenty-two catering franchises. He no longer works in the restaurants, but had heard that the Operators were going to be at this dinner and wanted to thank them personally for sharing the leadership model that helped him build his leadership skills. This young man had never eaten in a Chick-fil-A restaurant, but nevertheless, he was impacted by the generosity of Truett and others who serve Chick-fil-A.

Truett modeled loyalty, especially in relationships. He opened his original Dwarf Grill in Hapeville, Georgia, after World War II, and the employees of Delta Airlines and the nearby Ford Motor Company plant were instrumental in building Truett's first business. Some ate with him three times each day. For that reason, almost all Chick-fil-A charter flights have been with Delta Airlines, and Truett exclusively drove Ford Motor Company vehicles until his death. He also gave away Ford automobiles to Operators who achieved certain sale goals, an award known as the Symbol of Success. To date, nearly 1,300 Ford automobiles have been purchased for award-winning Chick-fil-A Operators. When the Ford Motor Company plant in Hapeville closed several years ago, Truett purchased the last car to roll off the assembly line.

Truett also showed great loyalty to those who served his company. While it is difficult to be selected as a Chick-fil-A Operator or staff member, once a person is chosen to join the organization, we expect to have a long-term relationship with that person. If for some reason we made a poor selection, Truett expected us to give our very best effort, to do everything possible to make it work. Truett's loyalty to others has been rewarded by loyal Operators, staff and customers. For decades, Operator and staff retention rates have remained above 95 percent.

With a clear purpose established, a challenging mission articulated and a commitment to core values determined, **guiding principles** are needed to act as "true North" on the compass of an organization. The principles serve as a guide to what the organization does, why it does it and HOW it does it. Every organization needs key guiding principles to direct its members and shape the behaviors that support the purpose and mission.

A painting of a mountain climber hangs in Truett's office. A gift from his daughter, Trudy, the words on the painting read: "No goal is too high if we climb with care and confidence." Truett had a long-term view of everything he did, and that long-term focus is a guiding principle for Chick-fil-A. He was careful, just like a mountain climber scaling a steep cliff, to help each of us find a foothold and handhold in the wall and keep moving upward with intention and care. We focus not just on what will make the most money today, but what will provide the best future for the business and everyone involved in the long term.

As previously mentioned, from the beginning, Truett closed his business on Sundays, and that practice has continued since 1946. Giving employees a day off to rest and to spend time with family has garnered both loyalty among employees and respect from guests. Truett, and later, his family, also decided to remain privately held and family-owned. Like being closed on Sunday, the decision to remain a private company may have slowed Chick-fil-A's expansion plans, but Truett wanted his business to impact the world, not just get bigger. In fact, he was known for often saying, especially when reviewing annual plans, that "we can't get bigger unless we get better." Knowing that stockholders would likely only want to grow quickly and not be as concerned with matters important to Truett, he preferred that the business remain privately held. One of Truett's favorite events was the Chick-fil-A Annual Operators Seminar. For Truett, this event was like a big Chick-fil-A family reunion. He invited all Operators, staff members and spouses to an all-expenses paid, four-day meeting in a nice resort. He invested this time to review the previous year's results and to introduce the next year's new product offerings and marketing strategies. Bringing together the entire organization at an annual gathering helped strengthen the culture by facilitating the building of long-term relationships between Operators, and Operators and staff. The event also gave Operators the opportunity to share best practices. Truett understood that such events would not likely be possible in a publicly traded company.

Another guiding principle of Chick-fil-A is that everyone will be treated with honor, dignity and respect. Individual differences fuel innovation. Respecting and honoring those differences strengthen the culture of the internal organization and create an inviting and hospitable environment for all guests.

Guiding principles serve to clarify and enhance the understanding of the overall purpose. Organizations that identify, commit to and continually affirm their guiding principles strengthen the foundation upon which decisions are made regardless of changes in strategy, core work and even leadership.

While creating a compelling culture is an essential

beginning for an organization, it's never too late to help your team or organization strengthen theirs. Start your strategy with the WHY through defining your purpose. Continue with the WHAT in developing your mission and then focus your efforts day in and day out on the HOW through constant commitment to your core values and guiding principles. With unwavering focus and discipline to the process, you can create a compelling culture for your organization. Given the great success of organizations that do, why would you not?

BUILDING A TEAM THAT CREATES A COMPELLING CULTURE

---

*If I were running a company today,
I would have one priority above all others:
to acquire as many of the best people as I
could [because] the single biggest constraint
on the success of my organization is the ability
to get and to hang on to enough
of the right people.*

—*Jim Collins, Author of* Good to Great

Even though it has been over 30 years since I completed the interviewing process and began my career at Chick-fil-A, I well remember my first days. My introduction to the culture of Chick-fil-A was powerful. I began my career in early November, so one of the first benefits I received was the traditional Thanksgiving turkey. Truett gave every corporate staff employee a Thanksgiving turkey in a rather memorable presentation. Long before email and voice-mail communication, we used the old-fashioned intercom system in our (at the time) one-building office. After hearing an announcement over the intercom, all employees headed to the basement of the building to receive a Chick-fil-A shopping bag bulging with a Thanksgiving turkey. My husband and I were newly married and very young, and we possessed limited financial resources. To say that I was grateful for that turkey was an understatement. I was so proud to go to my family's Thanksgiving dinner with the turkey that my boss, Truett Cathy, had provided. That turkey symbolized Truett's generosity. It was the first of his many generous benefits that I received when I joined Chick-fil-A. Years later, as the staff grew exponentially, for convenience, our staff began receiving gift certificates, and then gift cards, to a local grocer for a turkey. But the sentiment has remained the same. The staff still continues to receive this gift each Thanksgiving.

During my first month at Chick-fil-A and about a week after receiving the turkey, I attended my first Chick-fil-A company Christmas party. The party was held at one of Atlanta's nicest hotels and was a seated meal with assigned tables. When we checked in to receive nametags, I was surprised to see we were seated at table number one. I was as equally surprised to locate the table and find that I, a 21-year-old administrator, was seated next to Truett Cathy himself. Truett and his wife, Jeannette, made it a practice to be seated with new employees at company events. What a fabulous introduction to the Chick-fil-A culture! Within a month, I had learned my second lesson about Truett. Not only was he generous with his money, he was generous with his time. Title, clout or wealth mattered very little to Truett. He spent his life helping other people become successful. It is a value that I have seen repeated in his children and grandchildren. He used both his treasure—and his time—to be an influence.

Truett could have had dinner with anyone that night—another Chick-fil-A executive, an important Atlanta dignitary or even another member of his own family. Instead, he shared his night with me and several other new Chick-fil-A staff members to be sure that we not only received the very best possible introduction to his organization, but also to ensure that we learned important principles of the business directly from him. I surely did not know, and I don't think Truett could have imagined either, that one day I would be responsible for the on-boarding and cultural introduction for every staff member. I am thankful to have learned from the master.

TWO
SELECT TALENT

People decisions are the most important decisions we make.

Truett invested a lot into the culture of Chick-fil-A because he held a belief that *people decisions are the most important decisions we make.* That is true whether we are selecting an employee, a business partner, a mate or a friend. Who we decide to take on the journey with us can ultimately determine our success in business, marriage and relationships. Wise choices in the beginning provide a better chance of success in the end.

Understanding the WHY of an organization through determining the purpose is critical. Understanding WHAT the organization will produce, serve, sell is crucial. However, it is the WHO that actually produces, serves and sells. The WHO delivers! Purpose, strategy and tactics can be carved in granite and become somewhat static. The WHO is dynamic and ever changing, depending on the skills, talents, personalities, ideas and thinking involved.

Consider these six, must-do steps to
selecting the right WHO:

1. *Carefully craft the profile of the role you wish to fill on your team.* Identify the key skills and experience needed to be successful in the role. Think about the future of the role and skills that might be important later and include those in the profile also. Consider current strengths and weaknesses, and staff to the gaps. Use every hire as a chance to make adjustments to your team to maximize everyone's talent.

2. *Cast a wide net to search for candidates.* Source potential candidates from different networks to generate a diverse candidate pool. Differences can energize a team and introduce new ideas. Sometimes, fresh ideas from different perspectives can stimulate a breakthrough to a new level of team performance. Internships can create a pipeline of diverse candidates to fill future roles.

3. *Prepare for the interview with behavioral based interviewing questions.* Ask questions that cause the candidate to reply based on how he has performed in the past. It is a good indicator of how he will perform in the future. Avoid situational questions that ask the candidate, "What would you do if . . ." That is hard to know without actually experiencing the situation. However, asking the candidate how she managed a situation in the past should provide valuable insight.

4. *Thoroughly check references.* When properly conducted, reference checking can be the most valuable tool in the selection toolbox. It has been said, "Past performance is the best predictor of future performance." If that is so, then fully understanding someone's past performance gives you great information to choose the best candidate. Don't just verify employment, but interview the reference and ask for specific behavioral examples of the characteristics used to describe the candidate. Invest the necessary time to gain this helpful insight.

5. *Encourage the candidate to make his own careful evaluation before joining your team.* The best people decisions are the ones in which both the candidate and the team are certain it is a great fit. It is not enough for the leader to make a good decision to select talent. For long-term, successful relationships, the candidate must be sure it's the best choice, too! Be sure the candidate gets an inside look at your organization . . . the good, the bad, the successes and the failures. Then, try to talk the candidate out of joining your team. If the potential team member can be talked out of it today, that is better than six months from now, when you have both made significant investments into forging the new relationship.

6. *Commit to success.* Once you have decided and the candidate has accepted, commit yourself to the candidate's success. Do whatever is necessary to leverage the investment you have made throughout the selection process. Implement a development plan for the

new employee that leverages strengths that help the
team succeed. The development plan should include
opportunities to grow and maximize strengths, not
just improve weaknesses. Both team development
and individual development improve performance.
Revisit the plan often to ensure that changes in the
employee's work are factored into that plan.

Surrounding ourselves with talented people whose character matches our own, whose competency matches our
need and whose chemistry matches our team not only sets
us up to win, but makes the endeavor much more enjoyable.
At Chick-fil-A, we focus on these three Cs when selecting
talent:

Select for Character

One hot Saturday in autumn, my son and I had just finished watching a college football team lose a key conference game. I asked him if he knew at what point the team
had lost the game. He recounted missed field goals, ques-
tionable penalty calls and bad play choices by the offen-
sive coordinator. I, in turn, argued that our favorite team
did not lose that game on that particular Saturday; they
lost it three or four years earlier. Several years before,
this team had recruited three young men lacking the
character to manage the pressures of being a football star
in this popular conference. Early in their college careers,
each made poor choices off the field that brought school
suspensions. In a domino effect, the team suffered in key

games where these three players were needed the most. Add to that a lack of regard and respect for the program that had provided them an opportunity for a college education and, eventually, all three were dismissed or forced to transfer from the team only months before the season opener. The coaches had to field an inexperienced defensive secondary to replace them. The team lost the game long before it was played when the wrong players were chosen for the team. Entering the season with great talent at other positions, this team did not have the defensive secondary to keep their opponents from scoring. In the end, poor choices of talent in the beginning led to the team's key loss and sent them on a trajectory opposite of the outstanding season they expected.

Evaluating character is not difficult if the standard against which it is being evaluated is clear. Generally, a great place to start is to determine if the candidate can support the organizational purpose, mission, core values and guiding principles. Evaluate character in the interviewing process and through targeted referencing. Some characteristics to observe and consider are:

1. Did the candidate arrive promptly for the interview? This demonstrates that the candidate values the time of others and is respectful.

2. How did the candidate respond to the receptionist and other staff who are not considered an official part of the interviewing process? Some of the best feedback we receive comes from the person who drove the candidate from the airport or the receptionist who greeted the candidate at the front desk. If the candidate is kind, gracious

and respectful, that type of behavior is consistent with our culture. On the other hand, if the candidate is rude, condescending or disengaged, that would not reflect the culture at Chick-fil-A.

3. During the interview, are the candidate's responses consistent from interview to interview and consistent with responses in the application? Do the candidate's responses match the reference responses?

4. Does the candidate speak negatively of former employers or others? Such conversation would indicate a potential character mismatch.

5. Does the candidate display a positive and optimistic outlook? Does the candidate take responsibility for attitude, behaviors, results and outcomes or does the candidate blame others?

6. Does the candidate's track record indicate good judgment and decision-making or is it clear that some poor decisions have impacted the candidate's ability to influence others positively?

7. What do former employers and others who have observed the candidate's work say about his or her reputation? Past performance best helps us to understand what to expect in the future.

8. Share the company's core values with the reference and ask him to give examples of the candidate demonstrating those values.

9. Ask the reference if the candidate's behavior ever reflected negatively upon the organization.

10. In addition to talking with former employers, check references with other people to whom the candidate has been accountable, such as teachers, professors, coaches, boards and community organizations (i.e. Scouts, Little Leagues, etc.).

Character counts. In fact, in selecting talent, it is the most important thing. People can be taught to do a lot, but if they have poor character, skill and talent will not compensate for the negative impact they can have on an organization. Individuals with strong character can lead and inspire teams to achieve what talent alone will not. Choose wisely and begin with character.

Select for Competency

One of the most important decisions to make in any business is choosing who will work in the business. There is a clear difference in hiring people and selecting Talent. Hiring enough people is a good beginning;

> People can be taught to do a lot, but if they have poor character, skill and talent will not compensate for the negative impact they can have on an organization.

selecting Talent is an essential beginning. When I think of hiring **people**, I think of quantity. Do I have enough people to get the work done? Do I have enough people to run this shift? Do I have enough people to serve the guests? When I think of selecting **Talent**, I think of capability. Do I have the talent to grow the business? Will my Talent provide the kind of service that will attract more customers? Will my

Talent possess soft skills that encourage our guests to tell others about their great experience in our business? When I look for Talent, I am wisely matching the skills and abilities needed to grow my business with the competency of individuals committed to helping me. Creating a job profile to identify the necessary skills to complete a job is a basic approach in hiring for competency. We hire people for jobs. However, we hire Talent to grow our leadership bench and prepare for the future.

An Operator may select a teenager to clean the dining room today, but if he has selected someone with Talent, that teen may one day be a team leader, marketing director or even general manager. Strategically thinking about the skills needed for the future of the organization is key in selecting for competency.

When hiring people, the questions asked relate to how many hours they are available and which days they can work. When selecting Talent, the questions asked focus on the unique skills and abilities the applicant might have to meet the expectations of the role. Hiring people drives me to think, *How much can this person do for me?* Selecting Talent moves my thinking to, *How can I steward this valuable resource to grow both the business and the individual?* People take orders, deliver products and complete transactions. Talent identifies sales or service opportunities, exceeds guest expectations and creates memorable experiences. People and Talent are both trained, but Talent is developed and nurtured. People will stay with you to make a living, but Talent will stay with you to make a life.

One Operator who oversees two locations in an active, busy

university town, does a great job of matching skills, abilities and interests to the right job profile. In our restaurants, properly breading and filleting chicken to our specifications is one of the more difficult jobs. The Chick-fil-A sandwich is made with a filet that has been carefully pressed flat and properly covered with our secret Chick-fil-A® seasoned Coater. The pressing of the chicken breast is very important in cooking to the perfect temperature and, of course, the Seasoned Coater gives our chicken its unique flavor. This Operator hired several college athletes to work in the back of the restaurant preparing the chicken several hours a day. Since these athletes were strong, they did a good job flattening the chicken, known as "butterflying." Also, as athletes, they were very competitive, and enjoyed working quickly and competing against one another to prepare the most filets. These team members in particular would not have been happy working at the front counter. Front counter team members need a lot of patience to listen to guests, accurately fulfill the order and create an overall positive service experience for the customer. That is a different set of skills. The Operator also found the right match for those roles.

He knew that he could be more successful and his team members more engaged when he matched skills with roles. He was very careful to select team members with competencies that matched the roles and then let them do what they do best. He did not take Barbara, who is high energy, extremely social and engaging, and place her in food prep, where she would work by herself with little interaction. Instead, he placed her at the front counter or in the drive through, where she could interact with guests.

There are five considerations in selecting for competency:

1. Evaluate the demonstrated track record of the candidate against the job profile. Does the candidate have all or most of the skills needed to be successful in the role?

2. Does the candidate have the necessary experience and education to succeed in the role now, and will the candidate be able to contribute more significantly in the future? Does the candidate build your bench strength for the future?

3. Evaluate the interpersonal skills of the candidate. Is the candidate friendly and engaging? Conversational? Aloof and distant? Socially capable?

4. Consider the personal appearance of the candidate? Does the candidate present himself for the interview appropriately dressed, neat and well groomed?

5. How interested and committed is the candidate? Is the candidate enthusiastic about your organization and the specific role?

After screening candidates for character and competency fit, we turn our attention to fit within the specific team, department or function and select for chemistry.

Select for Chemistry

The periodic table of elements was not my friend in high school; in fact, had it not been for the tutoring by my boyfriend, I might not ever have passed high school chemistry. I am still fascinated, however, that the combination of certain elements creates a new compound. Some elements, when combined, are beneficial. Some elements, when combined, can be disastrous.

It helps to have a basic understanding of chemistry when building a team and selecting its members. It is important to discern which styles, personalities, strengths, weaknesses, attitudes and desires will combine well to benefit and move the team forward. The saying, "One bad apple spoils the whole bunch," can be true when considering the chemistry of a team. One team member who does not fit can be such a distraction to a team that the team fails to accomplish its mission. For the team member who does not fit, it can derail an otherwise successful career.

Admittedly, though, out of the three Cs of selection—Character, Competency and Chemistry—Chemistry is always the most difficult to identify. When selecting a team member from outside of the organization and having no opportunity to observe the potential member in a team setting, you have a few options. Consider the recruiting process for college athletes. College recruiters have the opportunity to see the player in action, talk to coaches about the performance of the player, watch the player interact with teammates at a practice, visit the athlete at home and invite the athlete to visit with coaches at the college or university. As employers, we have similar opportunities if we are willing to take the time to invest in the process. References of former employers, coaches and volunteer leaders of the candidate can provide excellent insight into the candidate's likelihood to fit the chemistry of your team. You can also invite the candidate into a meeting of your current team. Take in a ballgame or arrange a team dinner to include the candidate. Give the candidate the opportunity to select your team, just as you give your team the chance to help you select the candidate. This will ensure a win-win for the chemistry of your team and the successful addition of a new team member.

Ben was a candidate with an outstanding resume. He had graduated with honors from a top undergraduate business school, augmenting his business degree with a graduate design degree and 6 years experience at a top consulting firm. He had experience as a community service volunteer and led his fraternity in college. During the interview, he was able to answer most any question about his work experience. However, the conversation stalled beyond what he did from 9:00-5:00 every day. I really wanted to understand his leadership potential by understanding his personal goals, long-term interests and his dreams. It was difficult for him to carry the conversation and reveal his vision of his future. He came across as very one-sided and actually, a little boring. I tried to imagine myself as an Operator and Ben as my business consultant or having dinner with him at a company-sponsored event. In the end, it did not seem that Ben would add strength to the leadership bench that we needed in a growing organization, and I passed on Ben's candidacy.

Some people say, "We just didn't click." What I really think is that we fail to ask the questions or the candidate fails to answer those questions that help us understand how they are wired. When attempting to put together a diverse team who compliments each other's strengths, the ability to discern the connection is critical in the selection process. When the connection is strong, it energizes the entire team and environment. When it's weak, we lose that spark and it drains the team.

The selection of Talent is an art, not a science. Carefully understanding how an individual fits into an organization and matching the skills and talents to organizational needs is a craft improved and perfected over time. There is no scientific or mathematical formula that allows us to enter values and variables to provide the perfect output or solution.

At the end of every Operator interview, I always asked myself a question taught to me by a former boss: *"Would I want my three children to work for this person?"* It's a simple question that sums up my decision. If I would not want my children to work for this person, why would anyone want to work for this person? So I assess character first. Does this person have the character to be a role model to team members who work in the restaurant? Does this person possess the leadership

> At the end of every Operator interview, I always asked myself a question taught to me by a former boss: "Would I want my three children to work for this person?"

competency to lead team members well and provide a positive employment experience to team members and a remarkable experience to guests? Does this candidate have relational chemistry to be able to engage and support team members and guests of the restaurant? In evaluating candidates for the most important role in our business—the restaurant Operator—considering whether or not I would want my children to work for the candidate helps me reach a conclusion.

Selection guided by the careful evaluation of character, competency and chemistry has been a winning recipe for selecting Talent at Chick-fil-A.

THREE
SUSTAIN TALENT

Once you have invested heavily to recruit and select great talent, be sure to retain the talent, too. While in New York recently I visited a store that specializes in paper products made from repurposed elephant dung. Another store nearby displayed products—everything from bracelets to clocks—made completely from recycled vinyl records. Reusable, recycled, renewable and repurposed are all words we hear often about precious natural resources. It begs the question: What about the sustainability of people?

If we are to have the Talent we need to be competitive in the future, we must focus on the sustainability of people. Our Talent needs to individually be holistically healthy to position our organizations for future success. There is not an endless supply of talented people, which makes it even more important to sustain the current Talent. An organization's cultural health is dependent on the holistic health of the individuals in the organization. Consider sustainable Talent in three ways:

> If we are to have the Talent we need to be competitive in the future, we must focus on the sustainability of people.

Sustainable Talent is physically healthy. Wellness is a popular benefit in many organizations now. Fitness centers, personal training, nutrition counseling and on-site medical clinics are highly sought-after perks among job seekers. Leaders must juggle competing priorities, stressful schedules and endless demands. Encouraging good physical health ensures that our organizations are stacked with available and capable talent to produce healthy organizational results. Obviously, circumstances and health are different from person to person and some people have limitations. However, the idea is to provide opportunities and the environment for each person to be as healthy as possible.

Sustainable Talent is mentally healthy. Investment in the mental health of our talent pays great dividends. Rested minds are more innovative and creative. Stephen Covey's seventh habit of highly effective people is to "sharpen the saw." Mentally healthy people read, study, listen and observe to refine and perfect their craft. Promoting time for rest and renewal invites the opportunity for mentally healthy talent.

Sustainable Talent is emotionally healthy. Access to employee assistance programs, programs and activities for spiritual development and emphasis on healthy relationships inside and outside of the marketplace enhances emotional health. Emotionally healthy leaders manage day-to-day stress better, are more able to inspire other Talent, and generally make better decisions for the organization.

Imagine this Scenario:

Carlita always had been a high performing employee. She achieved incredible results while balancing a family of a husband and three children. On the weekends, between dance recitals, softball games and piano lessons, she also cared for her aging parents. It was becoming more and more obvious to Carlita that she was not going to be able to continue to "burn the candle at both ends" and successfully manage family and work responsibilities without taking care of herself. She suddenly found herself several pounds overweight and exhibiting signs of burnout and stress-induced illness. Not able to sleep well, Carlita was concerned that her circumstances were impacting her ability to focus at work. Fortunately for Carlita, resources were close at hand. She made an appointment for a fitness assessment at the on-site wellness center and received coaching for some improvements she wished to make. The nutritionist helped her plan meals that would better fuel her body to meet the demands in her life. She joined a group training session that put her back on track for regular workouts, and also received a customized plan to help her lose pounds and increase strength and endurance. The Employee Assistance Program provided a counselor to talk through some of her stress and pick up some sleep strategy advice. The work/life element of the Employee Assistance Program made recommendations to help with arrangements for her parents. Finally, the on-site childcare provider gave Carlita helpful hints for smoother nighttime routines for the children to help get the family to bed earlier for a good night's sleep. Soon, Carlita was back on top of her game, having lost 20 pounds and able to get seven hours of sleep each night. Her nutrition plan gave her energy for long days at work and home. Even Carlita's supervisor recognized the creativity she was bringing to the team and her work each day. The investment of the organization into Carlita's well-being allowed her to contribute her best work every day.

Organizations that want to sustain, not just retain, Talent understand the mind-body-spirit connection and nurture all three. Sustainability is defined as something that can be used without being completely used up or destroyed. Retention is simply just holding on to something. Retained people can be just warm bodies. Sustained Talent is competitive advantage.

FOUR
STEWARD TALENT

J ust like financial resources, Talent is a resource to be stewarded, not squandered. Investing deeply in selecting Talent requires accountability to the stewardship of Talent. If we are good stewards of financial resources, we are careful to plan how we will invest them. The same is true with Talent. To be a good steward of Talent, we plan how we will invest *in* our staff.

Stewardship of Talent requires us to provide performance feedback and management of that talent. Setting goals, providing clear direction and measuring results are essential parts of building a strong culture. Employees who have clarity about their role, confidence in their ability to do their work and the support of their supervisors are more engaged, and that helps strengthen a culture. When clarity of role is absent and feedback is infrequent, the culture suffers. Lots of organizations provide performance feedback programs and systems, but many fail to do so in a transparent way that tells employees the sought-after truth to improve performance and contribution.

The kindest thing you can do for someone is tell the truth. This is especially true when providing feedback.

Most every person has a shortage of truth tellers willing to say what no one else will. I am not necessarily talking about the kind of truth telling that says the tie does not match the shirt or acknowledging my bad hair day. I am talking about the kind of truth that says, "I have made a decision that impacts your work, your role, your team or your future and I need to explain it to you." Truth telling is what emotionally healthy adults do with one another. Work-arounds are paternalistic and damage most any relationship. Mature truth tellers have the other person's best interest at heart.

> **The kindest thing you can do for someone is tell the truth.**

How to tell the truth:

- *Don't mince words or confuse the recipient of your feedback by a long introduction.* The other person cannot hear what you are saying while wondering what you will say. Get to the point and give the feedback or state your decision.

- *Pause and listen.* Allow the person to digest your words, ask clarifying questions and even respond with an opinion.

- *Never assume you understand the motivation behind a person's behavior.* When communicating your decisions, only give feedback about the behaviors themselves and tell the truth about the impact of those behaviors.

- *Expect the best.* Truth telling provides critical information for someone else to make adjustments, change or even support your decision. Many people do change as a result of thoughtful truth telling.

- *Be prepared for the worst.* Telling the truth can end a relationship, but most of the time, it will strengthen it.

- *Always show respect.* Don't editorialize the truth or belittle the recipient. Honestly communicate the observation or the decision you have made and thank the recipient for listening to you.

Mia was a ten-year employee at a healthcare organization who struggled to understand why she was passed over again and again for a promotion. The truth was that Mia struggled to communicate a clear vision of her work and translate it into an actionable strategy. These are key leadership skills that Mia lacked. However, Mia's leader never gave her that feedback, nor did anyone else. Additionally, her leader did not give Mia the "last ten percent," which was that her peers felt as though she was too quick to take the credit for work that was executed as a team. Instead of providing her with this crucial feedback, her manager hired and promoted others over her as a work-around to her shortcomings in performance. Mia believed she was a top performer and had built solid relationships. She was confused by her perceptions of herself and the actions of her leader. Had Mia been led by a truth teller earlier in her career, her trajectory may have been different and the company would have benefitted.

Truth telling is an investment we must make in relationships—whether personal or professional. It takes a lot of time and thought, and sometimes, courage. However, there is probably not another investment of time that pays a greater dividend when done well. Most people desire to perform and achieve results. Most people want to preserve important relationships. Truth telling helps people perform better and often strengthens relationships. Likely, you will find that people thank you for telling the truth, even when they don't like it.

Another way we steward our investment in talent is to provide opportunities to develop and grow that talent. Each staff employee at Chick-fil-A has an individual development plan and budget. Employees can use the funds to attend workshops and conferences, buy books, participate in Chick-fil-A sponsored events and training, travel with a SERVE team (teams of Operators and staff that teach the SERVE Model© globally to other business leaders) to teach leadership skills in another country or a host of other opportunities.

Sometimes, being a good steward of Talent is helping an employee get to their next stage in life successfully. At the Chick-fil-A Corporate office, we have a key People principle: departments or functions do not own Talent; the organization does. So often, when we attract, select and cultivate great Talent, we envision that person "belonging" to us because of our investment. Sometimes, that is not best for the organization or the individual.

One Chick-fil-A Operator in Utah tells the story of how she learned this important talent stewardship skill. The Operator took her employee, Katie, on a trip to the Chick-fil-A Corporate office in Atlanta for a developmental opportunity. Katie was a key member of this Operator's high performance leadership team. The Operator envisioned Katie continuing to be a significant part of her leadership team and growing a future at Chick-fil-A. On that trip, Katie told her Operator that she really wanted to be a photographer. The Operator said she learned after many years that she needed to be a good steward of the Talent entrusted to her and one way she does that is to support and encourage her team member's goals and dreams.

Upon returning home from Atlanta, together they created a plan that enabled the Operator to encourage Katie and hold her accountable as she pursued her dream to become a photographer. The Operator helped her create a website and a Facebook page where she could showcase her skills and abilities. After doing some networking for Katie, the Operator found a photographer that was willing to hire her as his apprentice and teach her while she finished school. This Operator learned that sometimes to be a good steward, we have to let people grow and move to the next best place. Like this Operator, we sometimes want our employees to stay and fulfill the vision we see for them, yet, it can be just as rewarding to see them become successful in something they really love.

The Stewardship of Emerging Leader Talent

With all the changes businesses will experience in this digital age, the stewardship of emerging talent is a vital responsibility of today's leader. Young people who are now in school will enter the workforce working jobs not yet invented. They are a generation accustomed to a fast pace, immediate availability of information and constant change. These factors, combined with a whole new suite of skills and knowledge, position emerging leader talent as a catalyst of growth and innovation in your organization.

Emerging leader talent must be stewarded and nurtured to truly leverage all of this ability available to you. Without a focus on their unique interests and contributions and a clear development path, you risk losing them to another organization or worse, a competitor. This group of talent is looking for opportunities to add value and contribute immediately. If they cannot see the way forward in the early days of a new role, they will quickly be searching for a new one—inside or outside of your organization.

How can you steward your emerging leader talent? Consider the following:

1. *Give emerging leaders real responsibility early and often.* This group expects to be trusted in their job early. They may not necessarily yet trust you, but they will trust you more as you invest in them. As soon as you identify that a team member has a strength that can contribute, put it to work. The old adage "use it or lose it" can apply here. Emerging leaders want to contribute in a meaningful way as soon as possible.

2. *Ask emerging leaders their opinion.* This group loves to give input. You will get it whether you ask or not, but they feel more respected when you ask. Additionally, they have good ideas and bring fresh and new perspectives to any project.

3. *Create a clear development path.* You may or may not be able to map out a clear career path, which they also crave, but you can at least help them craft a development plan that will position them well for future opportunity. Involve them on cross-functional project teams, in opportunities to interact with leaders, and through attendance at internal and external events that will stimulate their thinking. Clearly articulate to them the possibilities you see for their participation in the business.

4. *Advocate for emerging leaders.* These new workforce entrants are looking for champions and sponsors. When they step out to act on their ideas, pick the best ones and publicly support them. They are from the "everyone gets a trophy" generation. They want and need recognition to motivate them and encourage them in their next assignment. And, as tempting as it might be, don't take credit for their work! Nothing is more demotivating to spend hours, days, weeks or months on something only for boss to come along and put her name on it. As a leader, hopefully, you already have what you want. Help others get what they want by giving them credit for the work.

5. *Allow emerging leaders to fail without it being fatal.* People learn by making mistakes. They can shut down, underperform and disengage in the face of failure if they believe it is fatal. This generation wants the opportunity to take small steps toward a solution, employ trial and error and have the opportunity to produce a winning idea. As a leader, one of your critical responsibilities is to teach others how to be successful in their work. Since success is a lousy teacher, you have to let people make mistakes, learn and recover.

During my first three months on the job at Chick-fil-A, I produced a recruiting brochure to help us attract Operator candidates. Although I had worked for an ad firm and had been a journalism major in college, I made a significant error. I misspelled the word "restaurant" and printed thousands of copies without noticing. I was totally humiliated and disappointed when my boss showed it to me. Because of my mistake, we were unable to use the brochures and were forced to reprint. I remember that the invoice for the printing was $5,000. It was a huge sum of money to me and I felt horrible about it. My boss did not belabor the point. He did not remind me continually. I made a mistake (for which I probably would have been fired in my previous job), and I learned from it and never made that mistake again.

As a leader, I tell my team that it is O.K. to make mistakes. Our goal is to be sure not to make the same one twice. Most all people want to do really good work. If we encourage them, advocate for them, propose a path, clear obstacles and barriers and allow them to learn by making mistakes, we gain their loyalty for a long season.

Macy was a fairly new and younger employee. She was making her first presentation in front of a large group of senior and seasoned leaders. She was well prepared, but no doubt, she had been anxiously anticipating the day for weeks. After an amazing presentation that clearly demonstrated her knowledge and expertise, the group began to ask her questions, quite pointedly. Two senior leaders asked her questions to which she, at the moment, did not know the answer. Caught off-guard, Macy was visibly nervous and struggling. Gently, her boss interjected and deflected the attention off Macy. This leader was advocating for his young talent just by helping her navigate an uncomfortable situation.

As I watched the situation unfold, I was not sure what Macy was thinking, but I was watching the leader and thinking that I would have walked across hot coals for him in the future. I took careful note of the technique, determined that I would certainly want to advocate and assist my own staff if the opportunity ever presented itself.

Emerging leadership is a goldmine for an organization, but the investment requirement from leaders is significant. Empower them, guide them and teach them and the watch what they can do for you.

We focus a great deal on the stewardship of emerging leadership talent and new leadership, but what about seasoned leadership? How can an organization reap the benefits and rewards of investments into long-term, seasoned leadership?

A Story of Missed Opportunity

Lloyd slumped in his chair with his head in his hands. As unusual as it is in today's corporate world, Lloyd had devoted himself to one organization for many years. Rising from hourly employee to senior leadership had taken him decades to accomplish, but his heart for business and his organization had always made the journey seem worthwhile. Recently, he was not so sure. Over the years, he had assumed ample responsibility and performed well. But, he began noticing that some of his expertise was being ignored in making key decisions. Without clear feedback, he was unsure if it was his performance as a leader, his competency in his field or his inability to manage the ever-present corporate politics. Whatever the case, Lloyd was growing more frustrated by the day and impacting his engagement as a leader. His company was missing the opportunity to receive the full return on the investments they had made in Lloyd during his lengthy career.

It had become a lose-lose scenario for Lloyd and his organization. Without a course correction, Lloyd became disengaged in his work and opted for an early retirement as soon as he was eligible. With some understanding of how to steward the resources of seasoned talent, the organization could have maximized Lloyd's contribution late in his career. Instead, after what had been mostly a successful career, he left with a bitter heart and without sharing important intellectual information and talent.

It's easy to be attracted to the newest trend, the latest version and the shiniest model. We forget that the older model might be sturdier and enduring. In some ways, it is like owning a home. For years, we might make improvements to the home, updating kitchens and bathrooms, adding additions and investing years in beautiful landscaping. Then, we see a new home that is clean, fresh and the latest style. We can quickly forget the years of investment we made in our present home, in our attraction to the latest and greatest. It's a stewardship decision. Maybe the current home has a sinking foundation, a leaking roof and rotting windows, and the repairs have become too costly. In that case, a new home might be a better long-term investment. However, sometimes, absent significant problems, the better stewardship decision is to continue to invest in the current home. Such can be the case in decisions about investing in people. This is what should have happened with Lloyd.

We hear lots of discussion about selecting leaders, growing leaders and leading leaders. Organizations invest in leadership development programs and Ivy League executive education for leaders. "Find more leaders" is often the edict given to human resources professionals from their organizations. Leadership is likely the key competitive advantage for all businesses, so we constantly seek it and value finding it and growing it. With so much emphasis placed on having great leaders, it makes sense to be a steward of those leaders. However, oftentimes, organizations focus only on the value of developing new leaders and neglect the development of seasoned leaders. A few will take their thinking to the next level and continue to invest in seasoned leaders. Organizations that invest both in new leadership and seasoned leadership will clearly create the most competitive workforce to win in the marketplace.

How can businesses be stewards of seasoned leaders? Here are six ideas to consider:

1. *Enable seasoned leaders to mentor other leaders.* Don't just suggest mentoring, but make this a key role for tenured leaders to pour their contextual and cultural knowledge of the organization into other leaders.

2. *Ask seasoned leaders their perspective about broad issues in the organization.* Over their long tenure, these leaders have observed many ups and downs and have likely grown relationships throughout the business. The organization can benefit from their "insider" knowledge.

3. *Don't assume seasoned leaders do not have new ideas.* Many of these leaders are attracted to innovation and because they are experienced, they recognize whether or not something is truly a new idea, or simply a repackaged old one.

4. *Tap into the wisdom of seasoned leaders.* Seasoned leaders have likely experienced many successes, failures and setbacks. Wisdom comes from navigating successfully through opportunities. Seek their wisdom when making key decisions.

5. *Continue to invest in the growth of seasoned leaders.* These leaders are often less encumbered by other outside-of-work responsibilities and available for assignments that serve the business needs. These leaders often help companies transition new functions. As long as they work for you, continue to invest in their growth for the greatest return on the investments you have already made.

6. *Respect and appreciate seasoned leaders.* Their contributions have likely been invaluable in building your organization. Respect and appreciate them late in their careers and they will continue to contribute to the success of the business in intangible ways.

Long career paths at one organization are no longer the norm. For the few organizations fortunate enough to retain tenured talent, it is important to engage seasoned leadership by leveraging their skills, abilities, experiences and business insights. Recently, at a company meeting, Dan Cathy explained that Chick-fil-A is entering its second chapter. He noted further that whoever is writing the second chapter needs to be somebody who was there in the first chapter. Seasoned leadership is first-chapter talent and it can help an organization navigate the transition to the next chapter successfully. Effectively stewarding seasoned leadership will not only contribute to business results, it also will strengthen the overall culture.

The Power of the "AND": Leveraging Both Emerging Leadership Talent AND Seasoned Talent

Smart organizations and smart leaders understand the importance of avoiding "either/or" choices as often as possible and instead use the power of the "and." Such is the case with stewarding emerging leadership talent AND seasoned talent alike. When we leverage the strengths, abilities, ideas and knowledge of both of these groups, we have the absolute best opportunity for success.

Emerging leadership talent brings a fresh perspective and, sometimes, even updated knowledge to a team. Their energy creates momentum for the group and their ideas catapult us to a new level. Seasoned talent understands the culture, key ideas and strategies that helped us to our current state. Often, they are the architects of the vision that drive the goals of the organization. They are the staying power—endurance, if you will. We find our sweet spot, the place where we are truly remarkable together, when we take the ideas of the past and their all-important context and connect them with the expectations of the future. It's that place where endurance meets momentum. It's the power of the "and."

Ruth joined my team a few years ago. At the time, she worked for another leader within my department and I had not generally been exposed to her gifts and talent. Recently, I had a very serious issue to tackle. I needed someone with more recent "outside the company" experience than I had. More than that, I needed someone who was an expert on this particular issue that could advise me, since I had never dealt with this challenge at Chick-fil-A. It turned out that Ruth was the expert I needed.

After quickly assessing the situation, Ruth immediately made a recommendation to me based on her prior experiences. Since this was a sensitive cultural issue, it was important for me to consider her recommendation in context of our culture. In this instance, momentum and endurance made a perfect match. Momentum quickly produced a solution and endurance measured it against the context of the unique culture. The result was an almost perfectly solved situation that protected the organization from risks AND also strengthened the culture.

As a leader and steward of Talent, your best results will come from leveraging all of the talent available to you.

FIVE

WHEN YOU MUST SAY "NO"

"It is kindness to refuse immediately what you eventually intend to deny." This was a favorite quotation of my mentor, Jimmy Collins. He used it as a teaching lesson about making people decisions. It was important to him, and to me, that we not drag people through a long selection process and delay what sometimes, we know to be true—that it's not going to work out for us to select the person. It is a principle that works for every part of life.

When I was a teenager, my dad promised to buy me a car for my 16th birthday. It was a very special type of car that I really wanted. I know now that I had no business driving a car like that at 16 (or many other ages, too), but because my dad had promised, my hopes were set on that car. My brother received a new car when he was 16, and I looked forward to my 16th birthday with great anticipation.

On the morning of my 16th birthday, I woke up early with anticipation of receiving my gift. My Mom gave me a box with a toy model of a red Corvette and the spare key to her "land yacht" sedan. There would be no sports car for my 16th birthday, and, in fact, no car at all. My hopes were dashed. I had already, for months, imagined myself driving into my assigned parking space at the high school in my new car. I saw myself being accepted in groups where I was previously not welcome because, now, I had a cool car. This car was going to be a life-changing event for me! I did receive a mode of transportation—a slalom waterski. I am pretty sure I kept the ski longer than I would have kept the car.

With certainty, I know for all kinds of reasons that it would have been a very bad decision to give me that car. In fact, I am so sure of it that none of my sons received a car for their 16th birthdays. They were given use of a family car with limitations on its use. The big difference was, from the time they were quite young, my husband and I told them they would not receive a car at 16. They had no expectations. I think they may have still had a glimmer of hope as their friends received nice cars, but we had been clear so that they would not be disappointed on their big day.

Telling people "no" is often a very difficult thing to do. Even more difficult, however, and what we often cannot see, is the disappointment that comes when expectations have been raised and then unmet. If we know that we cannot provide our time, attention, resources or an affirmative answer, we just need to say so. It is the kinder thing to do. This principle is true whether responding to our family members, business associates, clients or friends.

Have you ever been stood up for a date or waited for a friend to go somewhere with you only to have them not show up? In trying to be nice and say "yes," we sometimes fail to be kind just by saying "no." When I try to be nice, I care what you think about me. When I am kind, I care about you and your feelings. If the date or the friend says "no" to begin with, you can make other plans. However, when left to wait, the disappointment is two-fold. You missed the outing and also missed the opportunity to choose to do something else.

Integrity suffers and relationships are diminished when we don't do what we say we will do. To reduce disappointment and heartache in the long run, say "no" before expectations are created. The longer a situation

> **Integrity suffers and relationships are diminished when we don't do what we say we will do.**

continues, the more expectations continue to rise and it becomes much harder to say and hear "no."

Few days go by in my business life that I do not have the opportunity to make a decision based on the principle from Jimmy's quotation. My role at work requires me to tell people they will not be hired or receive a promotion, or that they might receive a smaller raise than expected. Sometimes, I have to share with people that the project they proposed will not be funded or that someone else will fill the new assignment they wanted. The saying that "bad news does not get better with age" is very true. The situation is never enjoyable, but it goes much better when we provide prompt, truthful answers. When we are quick and clear with feedback and responses, it allows the person to understand, move on and decide what to do next.

Not long ago, a staff member came into my office to receive coaching on a specific candidate situation. She was distraught as she really liked the candidate as a person, but she knew the role did not match her long-term goals and she would not get there pursuing this role. We could clearly see something that the candidate could not. I asked the staff member, "Do you want to steal her career?" At first, she was puzzled by the question, but then she began to understand. By placing the candidate in a role that was never going to allow her the opportunity she really wanted in her career, we would essentially be stealing her future opportunity. However, if we turned her down and redirected her to a different path, she might just get to do the very thing she was born to do. To hire her in our role, we would gain the benefits, but be a poor steward of her dreams.

The same thing can be true when there is a need to exit an employee. Nothing feels worse than constantly knowing you are not meeting someone's expectations. It's a miserable way to live and in an employment situation, if it cannot be resolved, then we need to help people find a new path to a better future. The stress generated by being unable to perform in a role at work causes physical, mental and emotional symptoms and illness. Often, the very most respectful thing we can do is help someone out of organization and into a situation where they can be successful. Many leaders are terrified at the prospect of having to terminate an employee. Sometimes we fear legal reprisal, but more often, we genuinely like people and we don't want to hurt them, so we avoid the conflict.

For employees that are struggling to perform in their role, consider the following steps and options to make the redirection process easier for you and your employee.

1. *Be sure the expectations are clear.* Again, most people desire to do well. Examine your own communication with the employee to be sure that you have clearly articulated the expectations and given enough direction to accomplish those expectations.

2. *Evaluate the individual's learning and development plan.* Do other learning opportunities exist that could help make this person more successful? Those opportunities might be expensive, but it is usually less expensive to train and someone than the expense of turnover.

3. *Consider another role within the company.* Sometimes, an employee is really not in the right role. He does not need to exit the organization; rather, he just needs to change roles. Identify the strengths of the individual while acknowledging areas of non-strength, and try to help him find a place in the organization to use those strengths. Consider an outside consultant who specializes in assessment to help you and the employee identify strengths and weaknesses and to recommend roles that may be a better fit.

4. *Redirect the employee to roles outside of the company.* If you decide that the employee is unable to perform the role and there is no other role to move him into, then exiting the organization may be best. Hopefully, by this point, you and the employee have communicated so frequently that this conclusion is mutual between the two of you. Utilizing outplacement firms,

even while the employee is still at the organization, can help him transition much more easily into a new role. Employees at all levels can benefit from this assistance.

5. *Own the decision and act decisively and promptly.* If and when you reach the conclusion that someone should exit, don't delay in taking the necessary steps. The longer the situation sits, the more impact it will have on the entire team.

No one relishes the thought of exiting employees. We have found these steps to be very helpful in navigating the process and treating everyone with honor, dignity and respect. Refusing immediately what you eventually intend to deny will ensure your credibility and integrity remain intact. People will not always like your answer, but they will respect you for treating them kindly.

SIX

WHAT YOU GET
FOR WHAT YOU GIVE

Great organizations have unspoken and unwritten promises with their employees. Most consulting firms call this the *employment value proposition*. It's what you get for what you give as an employee. I am not a fan of the word "proposition" because it is too close to the word "proposal," which is an offer but not a commitment. An employment value proposition or promise implies a commitment. When organizations achieve this level of commitment to and from their employees, success is much more probable.

Over the years, I think Chick-fil-A and the Chick-fil-A staff have enjoyed one of the most unique employment value promises in business. We ask a lot of our staff. We ask them to have complete dedication to serving Chick-fil-A Operators. As part of our on-boarding process, we make it very clear, as Jimmy Collins used to say, that there are no cash registers at 5200 Buffington Road and our job is to serve the Operator, whose team members are serving guests. Another favorite and meaningful reminder from

Jimmy was, "If you are not serving chicken, you better be serving someone who is." That is the essential role of the Chick-fil-A staff member.

At the corporate office, there are not a lot of rules. Instead, we are reminded to use our best judgment. We have found that if we select Operators and staff members with good judgment, we really don't need to micromanage the staff or over-consult the Operators. We provide principles and context to those principles and ask people to make good decisions within those principles. But we do also ask people to care deeply, serve ceaselessly and impact the lives of others.

Those three ideas and the actions associated with them have created an amazing promise between our staff and Chick-fil-A during the first six decades. For those associated with Chick-fil-A for many years, these words resonate as keys to how we might work together best, and what we can expect in return. There are three compelling principles to this employee value promise:

First, **we care about you, personally**. Candidates often ask me why I have chosen to remain at Chick-fil-A for so many years. The answer is easy: My absolute favorite thing about our culture is that we truly care about each other and the organization cares about its people. We don't just care about people's work—we care about their well-being. To that end, the organization has provided incredible benefits—some expected, some unique.

One of these benefits is attention to our physical well-being. Just as we have created menu items to serve the health needs of our restaurant guests, we also have provided opportunities for our staff to participate in protecting and preserving their health. In the on-site, fully equipped wellness center, Chick-fil-A staff members can participate in exercise classes, fitness assessments, personal nutritional coaching and group training. Through the Employee Assistance Program, staff members have access to counseling programs as well as work/life programs that assist with everything from elder care to college coaching to finding the best pet kennel. Our on-site café serves healthy and delicious offerings everyday. To help staff make wise food choices, the nutritional serving sizes are even printed on the serving line.

Through the Wellness Center, staff can receive a flu shot and participate in wellness events throughout the year. Many of the events are held in Chick-fil-A markets across the country where Chick-fil-A Operators and their team members also have opportunities to participate. The wellness program at Chick-fil-A has sponsored Grand Canyon hikes, mountain climbing on Pikes Peak and numerous half and full marathons, to name a few. And if it is rest and relaxation that you need to recharge your well-being, staff members have access to reserve a Chick-fil-A owned beach condominium in Florida.

While a vacation is a welcomed offering, for many of our staff, the most pressing need is for quality childcare. In 2001, Chick-fil-A opened its first on-site childcare center and has since followed with two more buildings and service to over 350 children. The childcare center boasts a 100 percent parent satisfaction rating and an award-winning natural playground.

This spirit of caring has permeated beyond services provided to staff by Chick-fil-A. It is also how we treat one another. We throw wedding and baby showers for each other. We attend funerals. We show up with flowers and meals for illness and surgeries and walk with each other through events both big and small. We swap stories of our children's sporting events and give advice on how best to support aging parents. We take the time to ask how someone is doing, and we take the time to listen to the response.

Our hope is that this promise extends from the corporate office staff to Chick-fil-A Operators and from them to their team members and then, most certainly, to our guests. At Chick-fil-A, we care about you, personally.

The second key principle of our employee promise is: **We serve one another**. If service to our guests is a hallmark of our brand in our restaurants, then for it to be authentic, it has to be demonstrated throughout our organization. On a typical morning, by the time I make my way from my car to my office, someone has offered to help me carry my belongings, several doors have been opened for me, the elevator has been held, and I have been greeted a dozen times. During the course of the day, someone will offer me a beverage from the café or break room. Someone else will offer the last chair in the room and go find another for himself. As soon as a volunteer is needed to greet a guest or host a tour group or simply bring special treats for a birthday celebration, many will raise their hand. While it is popular for Chick-fil-A staff, Operators and team members to serve and volunteer for non-profits and charity organizations, what's unique at Chick-fil-A is the way in which we

are willing to serve each other. It is
not uncommon to be at a company
function and see Dan Cathy, himself,
carrying plates to the table and seating staff and Operators. Staff members have found themselves with car
trouble on the side of the road on the
way to or from the office, and recognizing the car, multiple Chick-fil-A
staff members pull over to help.

> **Serving one
> another is excel-
> lent practice and
> preparation for
> serving guests.**

Serving one another is excellent practice and prepara-
tion for serving guests. A demonstrated track record of
serving and a genuine desire to help others succeed is a key
trait we seek in those we hire. People are often surprised
as they visit our office at the friendliness and care that is
exhibited. An attitude of service is woven into the DNA of
our organization and it all began with Truett's example of
serving guests at the original Dwarf Grill. Truett knew that
people visited his restaurant to eat, but sometimes, they
also came to see a friendly face. They came to be filled up.
But they returned because of how they were treated and
how he and his employees made them feel. Service makes
people feel honored, respected and special. At Chick-fil-A,
we not only serve guests, but we also serve one another
and that helps make our organization a special and unique
place to work.

The last key component of our employee promise is:
We impact lives. Recently, we were interviewing a candidate for a job. When we asked him why he wanted to
work for Chick-fil-A, he referenced a good friend of his

and said, "I have watched him become a better person since he started working at Chick-fil-A. He is a better husband, father, son, brother, friend and community leader. I want to work at an organization that impacts me and helps me be better in all of my other roles in life." Impact is somewhat the result of the other two parts of the promise, but it also originates in the growth opportunities available through Chick-fil-A.

At a company meeting introducing new digital technology to Operators, some of our staff gave a demonstration of restaurant mobile apps by ordering a pizza for delivery through two different restaurants on the mobile apps. One of the pizzas arrived within the time promised and the delivery person brought it to the stage in front of nearly 1,000 people. The group applauded and the delivery person was presented with a $100 bill as a tip. He took the microphone and introduced himself by the "street name" he was known as among the homeless in Atlanta. He shared that he often bought and gave away pizza to the homeless and that he would be using half of the tip to do just that. Can you imagine the story he told when he arrived home that night from work?

Chick-fil-A has impacted people in more ways than we can imagine; in fact, the stories we hear are endless. But one thing is sure: there is a multiplier effect to this. Those whose lives are impacted, impact the lives of others.

The magic of this employee promise to care about and serve others is that it is mirrored in Chick-fil-A restaurants by the Operators and their team members. That is the significance of being part of the culture, when, almost without words, behaviors become a natural part of the core of the organization internally and then are demonstrated externally to guests.

With the right people on board and the essential elements of a strong culture in place, the organization has what it needs to grow the culture within the team.

GROWING A COMPELLING CULTURE AMONG YOUR TEAM

Coming together is a beginning.
Keeping together is progress.
Working together is success.

—Henry Ford

Tim Tassopoulos, Executive Vice President, Operations at Chick-fil-A, often says, "Employers of choice add value to people, rather than extract value. Team members are a gift to be stewarded not an asset to be managed." That's a calling. The first step to creating a compelling culture for your team is to be assured of your calling as their leader.

SEVEN
CONSIDER YOUR CALLING

On a recent crisp fall morning, I had the rare opportunity for a weekday breakfast at a local restaurant. As I sat down with my coffee, I noticed a large group encircled around tables pushed together. I was the only other guest on the patio, so I could not help but overhear their conversation. It became obvious that they were younger retirees who gather regularly for breakfast at this restaurant. When one of the gentlemen stood up to leave, a friend called out, "You are leaving? Where do you have to go? You are retired!"

As I left that morning, the scene and the words the woman spoke reverberated in my mind. I think, sometimes, especially those of us who have been in the workplace for a long time, fantasize about such mornings and gatherings—days when we can sip coffee at our leisure and have no place to go. I don't. Please understand; I will retire from my job, but I will pursue my *calling* all the days of my life.

Christine Caine, founder of A21 Campaign and PropelWomen, recently made the comment during a Sunday morning message, "What are you going to do—retire and play golf? Really? As long as we are breathing, God has placed us on this earth for a purpose."

Many years ago, I found *my* calling was to help others find *their* calling. I have hope that I can use my journey as a roadmap for others trying to find their way. Perhaps, by studying the path I took, someone else could avoid pitfalls and stumbles along theirs and maybe glean an idea or two to help them along the way.

How do you discover your calling?

- *It's the thing that gets you up in the morning.* It resonates not just in your heart and mind, but sizzles in your soul. For me, it's the excitement I get as I think about both developing the people who work for me and seeing them achieve their goals and dreams.

- *It's what others tell you that you do best.* A calling draws upon your greatest gifts and deepest talents. I have a friend that some would call a house painter. However, I call him an artist. He does not just paint a house; he envisions the combination of colors and how the rollers and brushes will blend the colors to create just the right dimension of texture. When weather or product defect creates the slightest imperfection, he is quick to correct it.

- *A calling is the way you use your energy that makes an impact on the world, or at least your part of the world.* A friend of mine loved the experiences she had as a young girl at youth camp. She not only enjoyed all the activities of camp, but understood the impact camp had on developing her confidence and faith. She chose to go halfway around the world and start a similar camp for children in Africa. Now, fifteen years into the adventure, the camp has expanded to include team-building adventure experiences, climbing expeditions and team consulting to strengthen organizations. Her business has given her exposure to leaders from all over Africa and the Middle East and she is having a significant impact on people, all the while using her natural gifts.

- *It's the moment and the activity in which you feel God's pleasure.* There is nothing quite like the feeling of knowing you are doing what your were made to do. As portayed in the movie "Chariots of Fire," olympic runner and 400-meter champion Eric Liddell described it like this: "I believe God made me for a purpose, but He also made me fast. And when I run I feel His pleasure."

Unlike a job, which is for a season, a calling will beckon us for a lifetime. It creates an inner drive and restlessness when we live outside of it and peace when we are embracing it and living inside of it. A job is printed on your resumé. A calling echoes in your epitaph.

> A job is printed on your resumé. A calling echoes on your epitaph.

Consider your calling and diligently pursue it

Roberto had a calling. He desperately wanted to be a Chick-fil-A Operator. In order to provide a better life for his family, he left Mexico and his career as a doctor to move to the

United States. During the week, he worked as an hourly Chick-fil-A team member in a border town in Texas. On weekends, he returned to Mexico to cut and process sugar cane to help support his family. For ten years, Roberto pursued his dream to be an Operator.

Finally, Roberto received a call to come to the corporate office to interview for an opportunity. Even though the location for which he was interviewing was one of the lowest volume restaurants in the chain, Roberto was excited for this chance. During the interview, he talked about his calling and why he had sacrificed so much to follow his dream. His wife accompanied him to Atlanta, and while she spoke no English, she was clearly excited and supportive of Roberto's calling. At the end of the day, Roberto was offered the opportunity to operate an older, extremely low-volume restaurant located in a mall. At this time, most of the Operator candidates desired a new, freestanding location with its promise of high traffic volumes and growing sales. When offered the opportunity, Roberto turned to his wife and with tears in his eyes translated what he had just been told. She too, began crying, knowing that Roberto had realized his dream and stepped into his calling. What none of us knew at the moment is how Roberto would maximize that opportunity.

The location that Roberto would operate was on a short list of locations that we were considering closing prior to meeting Roberto. We were not sure that anyone would be able to be successful in that location. Roberto, however, was sure of his calling. He had waited ten years for his opportunity and he would not fail. In the first year, Roberto moved his family to San Antonio, where he would operate his first Chick-fil-A restaurant. During that first year, he increased sales by over 30 percent and won the highest sales award offered to Chick-fil-A Operators: the Symbol of Success, which is the use of a brand new Ford vehicle for one year. The second year, Roberto repeated that performance and, this time, won the title to the car. He also made the restaurant profitable and began earning the level of income to make the opportunity more attractive. After the performance he posted at that location, he was offered the opportunity to move across town to another higher-volume mall restaurant. Even more exciting was that Roberto had made his opportunity so viable, that we were able to attract a retiring Air Force officer to be the Operator of Roberto's original Chick-fil-A restaurant. Brooks replaced Roberto and also was twice able to win the Symbol of Success. After performing well at his new location, Roberto later was offered the opportunity to operate a freestanding restaurant and now operates two Chick-fil-A restaurants. Brooks also has since relocated and operates two freestanding restaurants. The struggling mall restaurant where Roberto began his career is still open to this day.

Thousands of lives have been impacted by one man's passion to follow his calling. Jobs were provided, scholarships were earned and dreams were realized among the team members and the thousands of guests that visited his restaurants. When people find their calling in their work, it changes everything.

EIGHT
PRACTICE SERVANT LEADERSHIP

L eaders at Chick-fil-A are called to serve. Without a doubt, one of the most significant factors in Chick-fil-A's cultural sustainability has been its commitment to the principle of *servant leadership*. Several books have been written about this topic, but I would be remiss to neglect my own personal experience.

Recently, I spent a week with leaders from another organization. These were truly some outstanding people for whom I have deep love and respect. But during the course of the week, while I was under their leadership, I noticed a certain anxiety building in me. By the end of the week, I identified the anxiety. It was the absence of being in the presence of servant leadership. During my time with these leaders, they practiced privilege rather than service. When there was a line, they were at the front. When we ate, they were served first. At events, they had premium seating. When others needed help, they allowed someone else to do it.

The absence of servant leadership that I experienced helped me to value what I may have taken for granted at Chick-fil-A. We recognize the tremendous responsibility not only to lead, but also to *serve* those we lead. In our culture, leaders are the first to arrive and the last to leave. Leaders ensure that everyone else is served first. They give deference to others and do not expect, nor accept, privilege.

I am reminded of Rachel, who understands servant leadership. Rachel, a veteran Operator and former team member herself, had just hired Trey, a brand-new, sixteen-year-old team member. At Rachel's restaurant, new team members first work in the dining room clearing tables and sweeping floors before learning to properly serve guests behind the counter. Part of dining room duty is also making sure the restrooms are clean and well stocked with paper products and soap. Rachel knows it's not a glamorous job, but it is very important to meeting high customer expectations. So every team member learns to clean the restroom properly during the first week of employment. Rachel makes it a point to be the one to teach them. Personally demonstrating *what* she expects helps team members to *understand* her expectations. Her efforts also communicate that she does not ask anything of her team members that she is not willing to do herself. Trey, like all the other team members at the restaurant before him, learned how to clean the restrooms alongside his Operator.

When Trey moved to the kitchen and learned how to do another difficult job, cleaning the fryer and replacing the oil, it was the kitchen manager, Will, who showed him how to do so properly. In fact, Will walked Trey through the steps the first several times he cleaned the fryer. When things became busy and hectic in the kitchen, Will always was willing to jump in and help filet and bread chicken, another unglamorous but important job in the restaurant.

Soon Trey earned Rachel's confidence and gained the responsibility for unloading the delivery truck and inventorying the products. Often, the delivery time was well before 6:00 a.m., but the operations leader, Roy, was there to teach Trey the process so that he did it correctly every time.

Rachel's commitment to excellence included a servant leadership model, demonstrating herself that she was willing to do whatever was necessary to serve guests and equip team members to do the same. Her example to her leaders permeated the servant leadership culture at her restaurant. Team members were willing to do anything Rachel asked because they knew that Rachel and her leadership team would happily do it themselves.

Servant Leadership Principles

During 15 of my years at Chick-fil-A, I had the privilege of reporting to an exceptional leader, who both modeled and taught servant leadership. He learned it himself from a Chick-fil-A Operator, who modeled it for him when he was only a teenager working in the Operator's restaurant. The impact of one Operator on one teenaged team member, who later became a senior executive at Chick-fil-A, has helped shape the behaviors of the entire Chick-fil-A chain.

This leader's example taught five critical principles of servant leadership:

- *Don't expect others to do what you are unwilling to do.* One of the things that I learned from my leader was that I needed to spend time working side by side with my staff. When they are in the trenches, I need to be in the trenches. When there is a challenging opportunity, I need to be available to help solve the problem. For years, Chick-fil-A has sponsored the Chick-fil-A Peach Bowl™. My leader did not sit in a box seat and watch the game, but instead, he worked right along with his operations team and local Operators preparing and serving thousands of Chick-fil-A sandwiches.

- *Acknowledge that every member of the team is important.* In traveling to Chick-fil-A restaurants with my leader, I watched as the very first thing he did was to introduce himself to every member of the team, learning names and asking questions to know them better. He rarely forgets a face or a name and Operators, team members and staff alike, often feel valued that he takes the time to know them personally. Like his Operator did for him, he remembers to thank each team member for his service.

- *If there is a line, be the last one in it.* Recently, I attended a staff-wide event that required a bus to transport us. As 1,200 people took turns boarding the buses, this executive was the very last one on the last bus. All the while, he was talking and visiting with staff members using the time to catch up both personally and professionally with staff from all areas of the company. Putting others above yourself is the hallmark of a servant leader.

- *Share opportunities and privileges with those who might otherwise never have the opportunity.* Not long after I joined Chick-fil-A, my husband and I were flying on a Chick-fil-A charter flight to our annual Operators seminar. As mentioned earlier, I began my career as an administrator. Truthfully, I was just glad to be able to attend the seminar. When we boarded the plane, we found that our seats were in first class. I watched as company executives passed through the first class section to the take their seats in the economy cabin.

- *Be inclusive.* Dan Cathy, who sees his responsibility to be a "curator of the culture," learned from his father and knows that inclusivity is important to creating and growing a compelling culture. He seeks opinions and spends time with employees in all areas of the business and particularly enjoys connecting with Chick-fil-A Operators and their team members.

At the Chick-fil-A Corporate office, there are no reserved parking spots for executives or private executive dining rooms. The 350-plus capacity childcare center is available on a first-come, first-served basis and is available to all full-time Chick-fil-A, Inc. employees. The 11,000-square-foot fitness center and the group training and exercise classes operate on the same basis. Award-winning Operators often have special celebrations to share their honors with their team members who have helped them achieve high goals. This type of inclusivity strengthens the culture at all levels of the organization. Individuals truly feel a part of the mission of the organization and feel treated with honor, dignity and respect.

A team's culture can grow significantly when leaders model and exhibit servant leader attitudes and behaviors.

NINE

NURTURE AN ABUNDANCY MENTALITY

Do you nurture an abundancy mentality among your team or display and role model a scarcity mentality? Do team members believe there is enough opportunity for everyone, or feel that opportunities are scarce?

When I visit my young friends in a remote village in Africa, they impress me so much by their ability to share anything. If given a pencil, they share it. If given a candy bar, they quickly calculate how many pieces it can be broken into so that everyone gets a share of it. They don't seem to enjoy what they have unless they are sharing it with others. Isn't it interesting that people who have so little are concerned with giving to others?

These young children have adopted an abundancy mentality—*there is enough for everyone and I have hope there will be more, so I can share.* The alternative is a scarcity mentality—I must hold on to what I have because the resources are limited and I have no hope to attain more.

In organizations, I see this played out most often when promotions are earned and awarded. Members of a healthy

> **Members of a healthy team celebrate the accomplishments of others, believing progress for some is progress for all.**

team celebrate the accomplishments of others, believing progress for some is progress for all. Healthy team members also believe there is enough opportunity for everyone and realize that success for one gives hope for all. A scarcity mentality is often prevalent on unhealthy teams. In that environment, team members resent the success of others because they believe that it limits individual opportunity. If someone else achieves a goal or dream, they believe that there is less for anyone else to achieve.

Remember the chip commercial that encouraged buyers to go ahead and indulge? Their message was "Crunch all you want. We'll make more." That ad appealed to the abundancy mentality within the buyer. There was no need to ration out the chips or save for later—the buyer was assured there would be more!

Great leaders have an abundancy mentality and they nurture it in their teams to strengthen the culture. Everywhere they look, they see opportunity for themselves and for others. They realize that success for others does not limit their own opportunity, but actually paves the way of success.

How do you identify an abundancy mentality in others?

1. *People who have an abundancy mentality foster other people's dreams.* Sure, they have dreams of their own, but they are interested in helping others achieve their dreams. They know this will make the team as a whole stronger.

2. *People who have an abundancy mentality have confidence.* They believe in a unique and chosen plan for their own life and know that it is not impacted by the accomplishments of others.

3. *People who have an abundancy mentality coach and mentor others.* They share their time and talents to support the success of others.

4. *People who have an abundancy mentality are optimistic.* They are positive in their outlook and rarely, if ever, complain. They see the best in others and celebrate it.

5. *People who have an abundancy mentality are generous.* They freely share their ideas, talents, advice and expertise. They are not concerned with who gets the credit.

Brent is an Operator with an abundancy mentality, and that same spirit has permeated through his team. He hired a single woman raising four children. She was recently divorced, received no child support and was having a very difficult time making ends meet. Brent was attracted to her beautiful spirit and was sure that she would share that same spirit with his guests. He could see that she just needed a chance. Brent hired her, trained her, and immediately could see that she was a difference-maker.

Each day, the woman arrived to work by taxi. Brent and his wife decided she needed her own vehicle and set in motion a plan to make that happen. He told the team at the restaurant what he and his wife were doing. The team contributed some money and the Operator and his wife covered the rest. They went to a local dealer and bought her a used van. Brent had so much fun presenting to her not only a vehicle, but also her independence. She has since taken it upon herself to drive a homeless man, who eats at the restaurant, to the shelter each day after she finishes her shift at the restaurant. She is paying it forward. Brent and his team are generous and practicing an abundancy mentality.

Leaders and team members with abundancy mentalities strengthen the culture of a team and exponentially increase the likelihood of achieving team results. Unlike those with scarcity mentalities who limit and restrain the team, these forward-thinking leaders propel themselves and the team into immeasurable success.

TEN
FACILITATE OPPORTUNITIES

Operators often thank me for their opportunity to be an Operator. I am quick to remind them that Truett provided the opportunity; I was only the facilitator. I have a friend who describes my role as a "blessings broker." Without a doubt, one of my favorite roles during my career has been to be an Opportunity Facilitator for Chick-fil-A. In that role, I have met some of the most amazing people, each with their own amazing story. Like Roberto, so many of them beat incredible odds to have an opportunity to operate their own business.

Growing up during the Depression and living in Atlanta's first housing project, Truett Cathy understood poverty. He knew that if he were to have anything in life, he would have to work for it. As his own story goes, his mother was the rock of his family, and he had a physically and emotionally absent father. There was no one to give him a start in life; he had to do it himself. He truly started with nothing but a dream and a willingness to work hard. Truett found ways to earn money at a very young age and his first entrepreneurial venture was at age eight. Truett bought a six-pack of Coca-Colas™ for a quarter and sold them door-to-door for a nickel each, making a five-cent profit on each six-pack. He delivered newspapers as a young teen for the *Atlanta Journal-Constitution*, paying special attention to service to his customers. Later, when World War II ended, Truett was honorably discharged from the Army and he and his brother, using their life savings, began their first restaurant, the Dwarf Grill.

When Truett decided to open multiple restaurants, he was not interested in the responsibility of each of those restaurants. He wanted to select people who would solve the problems and treat the business as if they were the owner. So he devised a brilliant Operator agreement that allowed an individual to go into business with him for a nominal investment and to share in the profits. Truett was not looking for investors; he was looking for leaders with an entrepreneurial spirit, strong work ethic and a desire to operate a business who simply lacked the financial resources to do so.

Truett was the original opportunity facilitator. He loved the idea of helping people get a start in life and then watching the return on his investment grow. It was a win-win scenario that did not just offer profits to Truett, Chick-fil-A and the Operator, but also to the millions that have been impacted by the generosity of Truett and Chick-fil-A Operators. As Operators grew their businesses, they became opportunity facilitators for millions of team members and guests. To date, over $225 million dollars in scholarships have been given away to team members through the Chick-fil-A leadership scholarship. And beyond that, dozens of Operators have provided their own scholarship opportunity for team members. One, in particular, has provided over $300,000 in education support to his team members. Sixty-five percent of Chick-fil-A Operators were once Chick-fil-A team members working for an Operator. Schools, churches, wells for clean drinking water, feeding programs and orphanages have been funded all over the world by Chick-fil-A Operators and Chick-fil-A Corporate staff members. Through a Chick-fil-A-sponsored foundation, LifeShape International, Chick-fil-A Operators and staff have taught leadership skills to business leaders in dozens of countries. For Truett Cathy, selling chicken was a means to impact the world.

Some of my favorite stories involve entrepreneurs who immigrated to the United States to provide a better future for their family. Some of them left deplorable conditions to come to the United States and most all of them left everything behind. One young woman who later became a Chick-fil-A Operator literally walked out of Columbia at age 16 and made her way to the U.S., later becoming a U.S. citizen. Another young man left Romania after the fall of Communism in that country. He, like Roberto, took over a difficult situation and turned it into a great future for himself and his family. One Operator was previously an executive in South America and survived a kidnapping. All of these Operators desired to work hard for the opportunity to do something they could not do in their home country—operate their own business.

For some, the opportunity did not come quickly. But what a difference it made when the opportunity did come. There was a young woman who worked as a team member and then traveled the U.S. for several years supporting the grand openings of Chick-fil-A restaurants in new markets. She helped Chick-fil-A pioneer its way into Southern California and, after waiting for years for her own franchise, now operates a successful restaurant in Orange County, California. Another young man started working at at a Chick-fil-A restaurant as a high school student. He worked for a different Chick-fil-A Operator throughout college, and post-college worked for another one in a management development program. Upon completing the program, he accepted interim manager assignments and was finally selected to operate his first location from one of those assignments. Finally, at age 29, some 12 years after he began his Chick-fil-A journey, he became the Operator at a new, promising, freestanding location.

All of these stories reinforce Truett's original vision of providing opportunities for promising entrepreneurs who just needed a chance to chase a dream. Were all of the Operators he gave opportunities to successful? Of course not, but there is no doubt that the Chick-fil-A brand would not be what it is today without the toil and success of so many Operators. Business grows and the culture is strengthened through the facilitation of opportunities for others.

ELEVEN
LEVERAGE LOYALTY

Chick-fil-A has a long history of high retention among Chick-fil-A Operators and staff members. The intense loyalty that has been cultivated is primarily due to the lasting relationships that are formed among teams and their leaders. **Loyalty is a two-way street. Employees will often be as loyal to you are as you are to them.**

David was 21 years old when he began his pursuit to be a Chick-fil-A Operator. He now operates two Chick-fil-A restaurants. He never forgot the time that Truett Cathy told his daughter she had a beautiful smile and that she would be able to do amazing things with that smile. It gave David a heart to help others have a beautiful smile, too. Over the years, this Operator and his wife, Gayle, have helped several team members gain a beautiful smile through providing orthodontic care. Gayle has even picked up team members and provided transportation to the orthodontist. The team members are under no obligation to David and Gayle. It is just a gift that they want to provide as a way of giving back for both the opportunity and the encouragement that Truett provided. David and Gayle get a lot of beautiful smiles as a reward from grateful team members. Needless to say, such care, concern and generosity has also bred deep loyalty among David's team members.

> While other organizations might only plan to have an employee for just a few years, we are hopeful to work together for years to come.

Truett was extremely proud of the tenure of leaders at Chick-fil-A. He credited much of the success of the business to the longevity of those leaders. He realized that turnover is expensive and constantly rehiring and retraining staff takes the focus of the business away from growth and innovation. Investing on the front end to make a great selection and effectively onboarding, training and developing employees is an investment to ensuring the kind of loyalty that increases retention.

New employees at the corporate office sometimes are surprised by the degree to which we value both results and relationships. We care immensely that the work is executed with excellence, but we also care HOW the work is done. This is not just important to creating a culture where everyone is treated with honor, dignity and respect, but it is essential to the long-term view that permeates our culture. While other organizations might only plan to have an employee for just a few years, we are hopeful to work together for years to come. That being the case, it is important to establish and grow relationships to strengthen the culture.

TWELVE
CULTIVATE COMMITMENT

Cultivating a spirit of commitment versus a command to compliance reaps continuous rewards, especially in employee loyalty. Compliant employees will do exactly what you ask. The employee value proposition with this relationship is simple and transactional. The employer pays the employee an agreed upon wage to execute agreed-upon tasks. If the employee is internally motivated, then he or she will complete work exactly as asked. If the employee is not internally motivated, then the employer will constantly have to remind the employee of the rules, requirements and responsibilities. I don't know about you, but that sounds like a miserable way to operate a business. Thankfully, there is a better way.

When a leader is able to get a team member to commit to an organization, the employee value proposition is something very different. The team member not only does what the leader asks, but also expends discretionary effort. The leader, in return, commits to the development and growth of the employee. This creates a cycle of commitment between the leader and the employee. The more the leader invests in the committed employee, the more the employee knows and can contribute. The more the employee contributes, the more committed he or she is to the business. That higher level of commitment translates to a greater contribution. The perpetuation of this cycle grows the business in exponential ways.

How does compliance play out on a daily basis? Employees generally do only what is necessary. Because selection is generally a weakness of the compliance-driven manager, most of the employees they hire are also compliance-driven and do not exhibit a trait of being internally motivated to do more. If the employee is doing only what they are told to do and only what is necessary, they are not looking for ways to further please the customer. If the manager is focused only on transactions and not on customer service and satisfaction, the employee is not thinking about serving the customers' true needs either. In this model, somebody is usually "chewed out" each day and turnover is frequent.

Commitment, on the other hand, looks very different. Leaders encourage employees to anticipate and meet guest needs, even when there is no procedure in place. It's more than just showing up at work on time, in proper uniform. At a quick-service restaurant, this might be holding an umbrella over guests returning to their car in the rain, changing a guest's tire or driving for miles to return an item left by a guest at the restaurant. In return, the leader takes a personal interest in each team member, understanding opportunities for growth and the team member's personal and professional aspirations and dreams.

Leaders who coach for commitment instead of merely

compliance invest more to prevent people problems rather than incurring the expense of having to solve people problems. Committed members of your team build the brand of a business. Compliant employees, at most, barely protect a brand. It may take more skill and intention to lead committed staff,

> If you want to lead a winning team, seek commitment from team members, rather than compliance from employees.

but it is also a lot more fun. Committed team members create committed teams and committed teams become winning teams. If you want to lead a winning team, seek commitment from team members, rather than compliance from employees.

I have seen both of these employee value propositions in action. The first one reminds me of a summer job that one of my sons had a few years ago. He worked for a lawn care business, where the boss required compliance and rarely received commitment. My son learned more from observing his behavior as an owner than he learned about maintaining lawns. Since we also were customers of this lawn care business, we had a unique perspective of understanding the owner as a boss and seeing the results of his management. Yes, it would have been far less expensive to cut out the middleman and have our son care for the lawn, but then he would have missed some valuable lessons.

Bob was the owner of this business and he was not very selective in his hiring, which was his first mistake if he was expecting anything more than compliance from his employees. My son's training was a one-week experience as a ride-along with his manager, Barry. Relationship beyond that was non-existent between Bob and his employees. He chewed them out regularly for failing to meet his and the customer's expectations and firings were frequent. Bob's insistence to lead his employees by fear caused them to be disgruntled and demotivated, and it often showed in their work. They had no commitment to Bob, the customers or their work. My son was partnered, for the entire summer, with Barry, which was fortunate, because he learned how to do things right. It also meant his days were much longer because not only did he and Barry take more care with the lawns they maintained, they often had to go back to other customers at the end of the day to correct the poor efforts of other employees.

One day, I had the opportunity to observe this in action. The lawn maintenance crew arrived for its weekly care of our lawn and did not know I was sitting on the porch. I watched as they mowed the small lawn and clipped a few shrubs. They were there less than forty minutes. As usual, they placed the bill for service under the doormat. After they left, I looked at the bill. They checked the boxes for numerous tasks they did not perform. It would have taken at least two hours to do all of the things they claimed. Unfortunately, this is the common behavior of employees who work for a boss who requires compliance rather than nurturing commitment. Employees do only what they have to do, and sometimes only what they can get away with, so not only does the customer suffer; eventually, so does the business.

On the other hand, over the years, I have observed Chick-fil-A Operators who are masters at nurturing commitment.

Their efforts are storied throughout the history of our company. Chick-fil-A Operators require a lot from their team members. Most every menu item is made fresh in the restaurant, including hand-breaded chicken, made-to-order salads, fresh-squeezed lemonade and hand-spun milkshakes. Additionally, since we are in the quick-service restaurant business, expectations for the speed of service are very high. Chick-fil-A's hospitality model provides for some service elements commonly seen in upscale restaurants like personally carrying food to the table, fresh ground pepper provided table side, delivery orders carried to the car, tables cleared by team members, beverages refreshed at the table and all served with a smile. All of that requires extraordinary effort by team members that are still part of an industry largely staffed by teenagers. Chick-fil-A Operators have done a tremendous job of cultivating commitment from their team members.

The stories include an Operator in Atlanta who has an extremely multi-cultural team with over 20 different nationalities represented. Understanding that the team needs to work together effectively, he makes a point of nurturing relationships by inviting them to his house for dinner. When their families visit from their home country, he often invites them to dinner as well. One of his employees from Kenya eventually became an Operator of his own Chick-fil-A restaurant.

Operators have provided their own scholarships for team members (in addition to the Chick-fil-A Leadership Scholarship offered by Chick-fil-A), taken their teams on outings to theme parks and ski retreats, provided limousines for their team members on prom night and a host of other generous gestures to build the commitment level of team members. In return, team members have rewarded Operators with unprecedented commitment to guests.

This spirit of nurturing commitment is not new. One Chick-fil-A executive often tells stories of when he was a team member in high school. Everyday, his Operator came into the restaurant and spoke individually to each team member, and at the end of their shift, he thanked each one for the work they had done. When this one Chick-fil-A executive left for college, his Operator told him that if he needed anything, if his car should breakdown on the way or his funds run low, to call him and he would come help him. Commitment to one another breeds commitment.

Commitment starts at the restaurant level, but prevails throughout our business. Corporate office staff members have the same level of commitment to Chick-fil-A Operators. As mentioned earlier, Jimmy's edict to serve someone who is serving chicken has been taken to heart.

Late one afternoon, an Operator called the warehouse at the Chick-fil-A Corporate office for a badly needed equipment part. Not only did the warehouse employee quickly locate the part, she drove over 200 miles round trip that afternoon and evening to get the part quickly to the Operator. Twenty or more years ago, Hurricane Opal came up the East Coast. In its path, Atlanta suffered a great deal of damage. At our office, we lost power and fallen trees covered our ¾-mile driveway into our property. For the most part, Atlanta was shut down on this particular day. However, a Chick-fil-A Operator candidate had driven through the storm to make it to our office for his interview. One of our Human Resources staff knew the importance of being at the office to meet the candidate. Her husband drove her to the entrance of the driveway and she climbed over fallen trees and debris for the three-quarters-of-a-mile trek to the building. By the time the candidate arrived, our fabulous grounds maintenance crew had cleared the debris and trees, but the efforts of this employee to get to work had been nothing less than heroic.

So how do these investments translate into success for the business? In Chick-fil-A's case, Operators have produced one of the lowest team member turnover rates in the industry. The Operator retention rate spanning nearly 50 years is 96 percent. The corporate staff retention rate has consistently remained at 95-97 percent over the same time span. Most notably, Chick-fil-A has experienced a sales increase of more than 10 percent almost every year it has been in existence. Commitment breeds commitment and produces phenomenal business results. Commitment among employees is a catalyst for growth—of the individuals and the business. Fostering people's dreams catapults the business into a whole new realm.

THIRTEEN
FOSTER DREAMS

The Talent we select to be part of our team brings unique abilities, perspectives, ideas, thinking and insights. If we are to maximize their contributions to our business, then we have to steward not just the competencies of the employee, but also their interests and their dreams. In our business, Chick-fil-A Operators hire many team members that are on their way to something else. For some, it is their very first job. For a few others, it may be the first step toward pursuing an opportunity to operate their own restaurant. As the NCAA ad says, however, many will "go pro" at something else.

Chick-fil-A Operators are excited to help team members achieve their dreams and they are so honored to be able to play a role. After spending six years working in a Chick-fil-A restaurant, Shelly left to work for a large insurance company in their call center. She continued to be a loyal customer of the restaurant where she worked and kept her Operator updated on her progress. One day, Shelly approached her former Operator with exciting news. She had applied for a job within the insurance company. The position was for a controller and she was under-qualified.

During her interview, she gave details on controlling labor in her team leader role at Chick-fil-A. Shelly got the job and it is her dream job! In a large corporation, it is in an area where she will also have job security and be eligible for promotions. Her excitement was overwhelming.

Shelly came to Chick-fil-A for her first job lacking confidence and skills. Her Operator saw the promise in her and helped her learn the skills she would need to be successful when she completed her degree, including how to control labor cost. Today, Shelly oversees the schedule for more than 400 people and is responsible for controlling labor costs, not just at her branch, but in three different states. To be a good steward of the talent entrusted to us, we need to know what the endgame is for our employees.

Haley has a dream. She wants to save enough money to pay her way through college and become a chemical engineer. She has worked since she was 15, earned the scholarship her company offers and is on her way to be the first college graduate in her family. Juan has dreams to own his own business, maybe like the restaurant where he is a team leader, or perhaps another opportunity. He spends as much time with his leader as possible to learn the ins and outs of entrepreneurship. Calvin is retired from his first career, but enjoys extra spending money, especially when he goes to read to underprivileged kids on Sunday afternoons. He enjoys being able to offer them a candy bar or a soda. Bonita is saving money to buy her first car. Roderick enjoys his job as a training coordinator and loves to see his team members excel at new skills. He finds pleasure in seeing them succeed. Sandy works to earn extra money to provide needed therapy for her special needs child and she takes immense joy in helping guests who need some assistance, too. Her dream is to provide the opportunity to mainstream her son at school.

While most people show up to work to earn a paycheck, all employees have options about where they earn it. We have the opportunity to engage their hearts by fostering their dreams. As a steward of the Talent entrusted to us, we receive 100 percent of our employees' efforts when they know we care about their dreams and desires. We receive their extra efforts when we help them achieve those dreams. When their hearts are engaged in their work, our guests reap the benefits.

To foster the dreams of our employees, we must know and understand what the dream is and be willing to encourage the accomplishment of it. Do you know what each of your employees aspires to be and do? Are you willing to coach and encourage their dreams? If so,

> As a steward of the Talent entrusted to us, we receive 100 percent of our employees' efforts when they know we care about their dreams and desires.

then you are on your way to being a steward of the gifts entrusted to you in the talent that has chosen to work for you.

Truett Cathy, who fostered my dreams, was known to say: "If you help enough people get enough of what they want, you will eventually get what you want." It worked out well for Truett and is a principle that has proven to work well for all of us.

ENGAGING GUESTS IN A COMPELLING CULTURE

---

*Joy comes from surprise and connection
and humanity and transparency and new...
If you fear special requests, if you staff with
cogs, if you have to put it all in a manual,
then the chances of amazing someone
are really quite low.*

—Seth Godin

"Mr. John," as he is known to the team members and guests at a Chick-fil-A restaurant in St. Petersburg, Florida, is a Raving Fan™.* After losing his wife of fifty-two years, the 76-year-old found himself depressed and alone. While sitting alone scanning the newspaper one day, he saw an advertisement announcing the First 100® event to be held at the grand opening of a new Chick-fil-A restaurant in town.

At each Chick-fil-A grand opening, the First 100® customers receive free Chick-fil-A meals once per week for one year. These events have become so popular that customers often camp out for a day or two before the event to be among the First 100. Recognizing the opportunity to strengthen the culture and grow the brand, Chick-fil-A has turned the camp-outs into one long party for the fans. Overnight guests enjoy a sampling of Chick-fil-A products, a midnight icedream© party, a backstage tour of the restaurant and live entertainment and activities.

John decided to attend a local Chick-fil-A First 100 event and, afterward, he was hooked. He since has attended over 50 Chick-fil-A grand openings. The Operator, who, at the time, was Truett's grandson, Andrew, became a good friend and Mr. John found himself a place to call home. He regularly visits the restaurant where he has his own table that he occupies most days between the hours of 9 a.m. and 2 p.m. The staff provided Mr. John with his own nametag that identifies him as a "Raving Fan™." Known as the "grandpa" of the restaurant, John found more than a place to get a good meal. He found people who made him feel welcome

---

* The term "Raving Fans" is described in the book *Raving Fans* by Ken Blanchard and Sheldon Bowles.

and at home. It is not uncommon for John to be invited to team events and parties.

John's passion for Chick-fil-A continued with each new friend he made along the way. Having worked for the Henny Penny® Corporation, which makes Chick-fil-A's fryers, John has been known to help the Operator make a repair when needed. Although, it is a rarity in the St. Petersburg, Florida area to have a cold day, if it happens, John is ready with his own blow dryer to warm the hands of guests as they enter the restaurant.

John's wife, Joanne, loved Chick-fil-A, too, so John took his wedding band and hers to a local jeweler. He was wearing a hat with the Chick-fil-A logo on it and asked the jeweler if he would melt down the rings and make him one insignia ring with the Chick-fil-A logo on it. Initially, the jeweler refused since the logo is trademarked, but then when he received permission from Chick-fil-A's President, Dan Cathy, the jeweler happily complied. He not only made a ring for John, but one for Dan Cathy, also.

Today, the 84-year-old sports a belt buckle he made from his Chick-fil-A nametag and continues to attend as many Chick-fil-A events as he can. He has made friends all over the country who, over time, helped ease the loss of his wife. Recently John attended a Chick-fil-A Corporate staff event, where he was invited to share the impact Chick-fil-A has made on his life. However, the real impact has been John's influence on Chick-fil-A. Operators, team members, guests and corporate staff have all been encouraged by John's loyal following.

Raving Fans™ Larry and Karen share a similar story.

While Mr. John found his local Chick-fil-A to be a cure for his loneliness, Larry found a new identity for himself at his Chick-fil-A in Kentucky. Recently retired and without children close by, Larry and his wife, Karen, were looking for ways to give back in their community. They, too, discovered a special relationship with the local Chick-fil-A when they camped out in the parking lot as part of the First 100 event. Larry eats Chick-fil-A, somewhere, everyday. If he is in town, he eats at his local Chick-fil-A. When out of town, Larry seeks out the nearest Chick-fil-A to enjoy his usual grilled nuggets and fruit cup meal along with a cup of icedream$^{©}$.

A true ambassador of Chick-fil-A restaurants, Larry often buys meals at Chick-fil-A only to give them away. Most importantly, Larry became an encourager and cheerleader to the Operator and the team at his local Chick-fil-A. He is known for sending a birthday card to every team member and bringing homemade treats into the restaurant to share with the team members. Not only does Larry help the Operator by giving her constructive feedback when something is wrong, he lets her know when it is right, too. Most importantly, he tells others about his great experiences at Chick-fil-A.

As a Chick-fil-A Raving Fan™, Larry has cleared trays, mopped floors and wiped tables when he saw the staff in the restaurant needing help. Today, Larry carries a card proudly proclaiming his new identity: Chick-fil-A Raving Fan™. While guests at some restaurants and retail establishments are concerned about free gifts, discounts and coupons and anything else they can get, Larry is more concerned with what he can give.

Raving Fans™ like John and Larry have helped Chick-fil-A, as Dan Cathy says, "grow a small company." To grow and yet, at the same time, remain small sounds like a contradiction. However, it is Chick-fil-A's desire to nurture the spirit of such a concept so that guests and employees alike will enjoy the unique Chick-fil-A experience for decades— even generations—to come. Maintaining a small-company feel among the guests is a strategic cultural imperative at Chick-fil-A.

FOURTEEN

TREAT EVERYONE WITH HONOR, DIGNITY AND RESPECT

Chick-fil-A's hospitality policy is to treat everyone with honor, dignity and respect. Operators have demonstrated this continuously for decades. Truett encouraged them for years to not only treat guests and others as we want to be treated, but to treat them as *they* want to be treated.

One Operator had an opportunity to help a guest, who had been struggling financially, make Valentine's Day special for his wife. As a frequent guest of the local Chick-fil-A, the guest explained his plight to the Operator. The Operator told him to bring his wife in on Valentine's Day and he would treat them to dinner. The guest brought his wife in and, to their surprise, a table, covered with a lovely tablecloth and accented with candles and fresh flowers, was awaiting them. A server dressed in a tuxedo served the couple. Not many years later, when the young man's wife died unexpectedly, he recalled the special night that his local Operator created for them, how he was treated kindly, and how he now held with him a happy memory during that financially challenging time.

At another restaurant, a homeless man entered a Chick-fil-A restaurant looking for something to eat. In many businesses, a homeless person would be asked to leave and sent back to the street. Instead, the Operator gave him something to eat and realized that he was not dressed warmly enough for the freezing temperatures. He passed on his own gloves to the man as he headed on his way. But the man left with more than a meal and warm gloves. He left with honor, dignity and respect.

Several key actions consistently executed in Chick-fil-A restaurants have contributed to a culture that supports the promise that everyone should be treated with honor, dignity and respect. These include the response of "My pleasure," making Second-Mile Service second nature and creating remarkable experiences for guests. The actions help create and strengthen a compelling culture among guests.

FIFTEEN

AUTHENTICALLY DEMONSTRATE "IT'S MY PLEASURE!"

Signature service is an important key to building brand loyalty among customers. At Chick-fil-A, we believe that it is a privilege to serve guests, not a duty. Horst Schultze, formerly of the Ritz Carlton Hotel Group, attracted an intensely loyal following of guests by focusing on signature service. He motivated the employees of the Ritz Carlton by reminding them daily that they were "Ladies and Gentlemen serving Ladies and Gentlemen." He nurtured this loyal following of guests through unexpected, exceptional service followed by the phrase, "My pleasure." As Truett dreamed of a service model in his restaurants far beyond anything a guest would expect in a quick-service restaurant, he remembered the Ritz Carlton experience. While he rarely veered from his entrepreneurial mindset to present an edict to the chain, he did in this case. He taught Operators and staff alike to respond to a "thank you" with "It's my pleasure!" For ten years, Truett stood at the annual Operators' Seminar and reminded Operators and staff of his expectation of the "my pleasure" response. While it took a while for this to become the norm in all Chick-fil-A restaurants, it now is a standard and crucial element Operators and their team members use to focus on serving guests. The phrase did not just become required nomenclature at Chick-fil-A; it became a sincere response of the true service spirit of Chick-fil-A.

The language we use with guests can be a differentiator in our business and it certainly impacts perception of the brand and the people who work for it. The Four Seasons Hotels use the phrase "fully committed" to describe when no rooms are available. They don't say, "no vacancy" or "sold out." In that simple phrase, the guest is informed that the Four Seasons is fully committed to serving their guests and if they have no rooms to offer on this stay, they hope you will know they are fully committed to serving you during a future stay.

The "my pleasure" phrase has become more common in the service industry, especially at higher-priced retail outlets and restaurants. However, many loyal guests of Chick-fil-A, or Raving Fans, automatically think of Chick-fil-A when they hear the phrase. It is so much a part of my normal responses, that I use it often. I love when someone hears me and remarks, "You work for Chick-fil-A, don't you?"

Most importantly, "It's My Pleasure!" is only the language we have chosen to express the spirit of gratitude we have for our guests and an opportunity to serve them. While Truett requested the use of the phrase, he could not choose the spirit with which those words are spoken. Chick-fil-A Operators have selected extraordinary Talent and taught them not only the phrase, but the signature service to deliver alongside the statement. Through the teaching of the language and the principles, team members are able to exceed guest expectations and clearly convey gratitude for the guest choosing Chick-fil-A.

SIXTEEN

MAKE SECOND-MILE SERVICE SECOND NATURE

Second-Mile Service is Chick-fil-A's hospitality model. Truett built Chick-fil-A on Biblical principles, which he believed were also good business principles, and Dan Cathy and his siblings have not swayed from that foundation. Several years ago, Dan sought to explain the level of service he expected in Chick-fil-A restaurants by referring to a scriptural reference found in Matthew 5:41. In the Sermon on the Mount, Jesus says, "If a soldier forces you to carry his pack for one mile, carry it for two." It was common in those days for a Roman soldier to conscript a Jewish citizen to carry his pack for one mile. As was the law, the soldier could not require the Jewish citizen to carry it more than a mile as the pack often weighed 100 pounds or more. Jesus was teaching how to influence others even among enemies. However, there was an important point to the principle. The act could not be prescriptive and only behavioral. The gesture is most influential when it comes from the heart.

In most restaurants, going the first mile is getting the

order correct and serving fresh, correctly prepared food. To go the second mile for a guest, a team member delivers the order to the table, greets customers with a smile and by name and knows the orders of frequent customers. Chick-fil-A Operators are experts in adopting this principle to match both their personal style and the personality of their restaurant. Many Operators keep a supply of umbrellas handy and escort guests to and from the car in the rain. Some team members have served guests in remarkable ways by changing tires in the parking lot, helping push disabled vehicles out of the drive-through lane and even driving dozens of miles to return a lost wallet or cell phone. They have dug through dumpsters to find accidentally discarded dental appliances and they have made it their passion to surprise and delight customers in unexpected ways.

An exhausted Sarah pulled into the drive-through at her local Chick-fil-A restaurant. Her favorite reason for coming to this particular Chick-fil-A is that she can place her order in the drive-through for herself and her three-year old and then park and come in to find a table already set with a high chair and placemat. She does not have to stand in line to place her order juggling the three-month-old and trying to hold the hand of the three-year-old. After a morning of doctor appointments and visits to prospective preschools, her three year-old needed something to eat and an opportunity to stretch her legs in the indoor playground. Having dodged raindrops all day, Sarah was exceptionally pleased when team member Hannah met her at the car with an umbrella to help Sarah get her two little ones into the restaurant. By the time Sarah made it to the table and got everyone settled, their food was ready. As her little girl burned up energy on the playground, Sarah reflected on the exceptional experience and service she received. It certainly was not what is expected at a quick-service restaurant, but it is what she has come to expect at Chick-fil-A.

Marcus, a sales rep, eats at his local Chick-fil-A almost everyday. They know his name and his order: a spicy chicken sandwich, no pickles, with coleslaw and a large lemonade. A team member enters the order as soon as they see his car drive into the parking lot. Most days, his order makes it to the register just as he steps up to pay. In a hurry to get to his next sales call, Marcus is grateful for the personalized Second-Mile service. Advances in digital technology will soon allow Marcus and other guests to use a mobile app to order and pay for their food from work, home or on the road and have it waiting for them when they arrive at the restaurant.

Allowing guests to customize food orders is common and expected in most quick-service restaurants; however, customized and personal service goes beyond great service and helps to create a compelling culture among guests. At

Chick-fil-A, this has created some memorable interactions among the guests. Operators have witnessed guests clearing trays and packaging for other guests!

While the focus of our hospitality is in the restaurants, Operators, guests and fellow staff experience some of the same elements of Second-Mile Service at our corporate office. It is not uncommon to be in the café and have someone offer to "refresh your beverage" or return your trays to the dish room. Doors are held and courtesies are extended consistently. If a principle is going to be a pillar of an organizational culture, behaviors must be consistent and delivered in all areas of the company, corporate office and restaurants alike.

Because the concept of Second-Mile Service is a principle and a key component of a strategy, rather than an exhaustive, prescriptive list of behaviors, Operators and team members alike are constantly finding new ways to deliver their own brand of Second-Mile Service. In short, organizations that go the second mile treat customers as friends and family. When Second-Mile Service originates from the heart, it truly *is* a pleasure and a behavior that creates a compelling culture among guests. Our goal at Chick-fil-A is to make Second-Mile Service second nature.

> When Second-Mile Service originates from the heart, it truly *is* a pleasure and a behavior that creates a compelling culture among guests.

SEVENTEEN
CREATE REMARKABLE EXPERIENCES

Another key to leveraging talent and culture to create enduring impact among guests is to provide unexpected fun and remarkable experiences. Anyone can provide a meal, but an experience is unique, memorable and, at Chick-fil-A, should be remarkable. Chick-fil-A has created a loyal following through experiences designed to surprise and delight the guests. The First 100 event at Chick-fil-A grand openings is one of those experiences, with the highlight being an up-close and personal "Backstage Tour" of the new Chick-fil-A restaurant. Here, guests are treated to a view of chicken being prepared and hand-breaded in the restaurants. They watch as fresh produce is assembled into salads. They see the premium products Chick-fil-A uses, such as Hershey's© chocolate syrup and Oreo© cookies. They watch as lemons are fresh squeezed for the lemonade and sometimes are even able to make their own icedream© cone.

Thousands of Chick-fil-A Raving Fans™ visit the Chick-fil-A Corporate office in Atlanta each year to experience an opportunity to go behind the scenes at the corporate office. They view memorabilia of Chick-fil-A's past, interact with Chick-fil-A staff, peek into future projects in the innovation lab and even snap a few pictures on a life-sized cow billboard.

When schoolchildren visit Truett's office, one of their takeaways is a ruler, similar to the ones Truett himself used to give away. The ruler is printed with the words of the "Golden Rule": *Do unto others as you would have them to do unto you.* Those words are best exemplified in the actions and behaviors of Chick-fil-A Operators and their amazing team members as they create remarkable guest experiences.

Chick-fil-A's specialty is events that bring families together. In February each year, hundreds of Chick-fil-A Operators promote "Daddy/Daughter Date Night." Little girls dress up and accompany their dads to Chick-fil-A where they often find tablecloth-covered, candlelit tables, strolling violinists and parking lot carriage rides awaiting their arrival. Such events create fond memories of Chick-fil-A and create enduring impact for guests.

Alyssa remembers the first time her father escorted her to Daddy/Daughter Date Night at Chick-fil-A. At eleven years old and in her first year of middle school, she was having difficulties with the harder classwork and with feeling she didn't fit in with the other girls. It seemed almost everyone but Alyssa belonged to a group. Her dad, Ryan, had noticed that Alyssa had been struggling and very quiet for several weeks. When he saw the Facebook post from his favorite Chick-fil-A advertising Daddy/Daughter Date Night, he hopped online and registered for them to attend. When the big night came, Ryan dressed in a sport coat and tie and Alyssa wore a new red dress that Lori, her mom, helped her pick out for the special night with her dad.

Upon arriving at the restaurant, a stretch limousine was in the parking lot to drive the guests around the shopping center lot where the Chick-fil-A is located. Inside, the Chick-fil-A cow, dressed in a tuxedo, presented Alyssa with a red rose. Tablecloths and fresh flowers adorned the tables along with special placemats that prompted meaningful conversation between a dad and his daughter. That evening with her dad reminded Alyssa that, to her dad and family, she was a treasure. She and her dad were able to talk about her troubled heart. They left Chick-fil-A that night with not only memories of a delightful experience, but also with a strengthened relationship and a path to future vital communication between a dad and his young daughter. Daddy/Daughter Date Night became a tradition for Alyssa and her dad. Now that she is in college, she occasionally still will make the trip home and, for old time's sake, join her dad for that special night at the local Chick-fil-A. He still brings her a rose.

Hunter is an Operator who truly loves his guests. Each day as he walks through his restaurant, he looks for ways to connect with guests so that they feel at home and want to return again and again. He uses his natural strengths of conversation and humor and his background in national brand product sales to engage. An avid Green Bay Packers fan, Hunter spotted a guest in his restaurant wearing Packers attire. He learned that the guest was traveling through his town because his flight had been canceled and his only option to get home was a long drive. The guest stopped at Chick-fil-A expecting to enjoy a great meal, but he also received something more: a big dose of encouragement from Hunter.

A few weeks after the guest visited Hunter's restaurant, Hunter received a package containing—you guessed it—Packers memorabilia! The enclosed note expressed the guest's gratitude to Hunter for his engagement and connection. Unbeknownst to Hunter, this guest was a having a particularly difficult day and week and his visit to Chick-fil-A had been a highlight to his trip. Hunter's encouragement and conversation had lifted his spirits and made the rest of his long journey home much more enjoyable. Additionally, he told Hunter that their interaction reminded him how much he loved his own job and how important it is to include fun in the work he does.

The same Operator who gave away his gloves to the homeless man also gave away hundreds of Chick-fil-A meals to motorists stranded in a snowstorm near his restaurant. He also allowed employees and guests to spend the night in the restaurant since they were unable to drive home. The next morning the employees prepared one thousand Chick-fil-A biscuits to be shared with the stranded motorists still stuck on the highway.

A kind word, a generous gesture, an inviting smile and a warm handshake can have an immeasurable influence on the people around us. That kind of influence creates a compelling culture among guests that keeps them returning again and again.

CONCLUSION

LEVERAGE TALENT AND CULTURE TO CREATE ENDURING IMPACT

For us, in our quest to impact lives, selling chicken is only a means to the end. We sell chicken, but we are truly in the People business. A compelling culture grows in the big events, but mostly, it flourishes in the smallest of gestures consistently applied and executed again and again. Oftentimes, it starts with the vision of just one person and then the vision is caught within the passion of the hearts that live out that vision. It was true when Truett opened the Dwarf Grill in 1946. It is true today as the chain approaches 2,000 restaurants and over $6 billion in sales. And because culture is always evolving, we hope this principle follows us far into the future.

Every Thanksgiving, I receive a text message from one of the leaders in our company. It simply says, "Have a great Thanksgiving. I am grateful for you." At Chick-fil-A, we have grown a compelling culture by living life together. We celebrate joys with one another and we grieve losses together. We work hard together and we play and serve together. We grow relationships with guests and each other, one connection at a time. We engage the hearts of the staff, to better serve Operators and engage the hearts of their team members so that they can also engage the hearts of their guests.

Patricia is an almost daily guest at Sam's Chick-fil-A restaurant, often dine-in, but sometimes just a sweet tea in the drive-through. As with Ray, 40 years before at Truett's restaurant, Sam and his team not only knew Patricia's name and order they also know her story. When Sam first opened over 20 years ago, Patricia was one of his first guests. The playground was frequented by Patricia's two children, Dana and Kevin, who are now grown with young children of their own. They made memories together over nuggets and waffle fries, Tuesday kids' nights with the Chick-fil-A cows and Monday spirit nights for the local school. She and her husband, Richard, had a standing Saturday morning breakfast date until he passed away unexpectedly a few years ago. When Richard died, Sam sent food from the restaurant and the team members sent sympathy cards.

When Patricia's kids were in high school, Sam's restaurant supported their marching band and Richard and Dana made "Daddy/Daughter Date Night" a yearly tradition. When Kevin decided to apply for his first job, there was no question where he wanted to work. Sam invested in Kevin and he continued working for Chick-fil-A while away at college. When Kevin needed time off to study for exams or to go on a service trip to an orphanage in Mexico, Sam accommodated. When Sam needed a truck unloaded at 5:00 a.m., Kevin was the first to arrive. On prom night, not only did Sam arrange the schedule for team members to attend, he rented a limousine to carry all of his juniors and seniors to the prom. He both appreciated them and wanted them safe. Kevin and his date, Lynn, enjoyed their first-ever limo ride.

Dana and her four young children regularly eat at Sam's restaurant now, too. His team is especially attentive in helping her special-needs child when they visit. The restaurant's Marketing Director, Joyce, has her own special way to get little Tess to smile, even when no one else can. Dana's moms' playgroup meets at the restaurant every Friday morning. Sam holds a table for them. They love to take their children there because the playground is always clean and the kids' meals feature healthy selections such as grilled nuggets, applesauce and milk.

Kevin continued to work and gain Chick-fil-A experience. The start Sam gave him proved to be beneficial and after college, Kevin became a Chick-fil-A Operator himself. He married his prom date, Lynn, and they are raising three children who already have the response of "It's my pleasure" as part of their vocabulary.

After a lot of work and some lean years making his way, Kevin recently opened a brand new Chick-fil-A restaurant in a growing community. Carrying on traditions he learned from Sam, he rented a limo to take his high school seniors to a graduation dinner last spring. He still sees Sam at Operator team meetings and outings and asks his advice on growing his business. Sam reminds him: "Do what Truett did: love your guests and love your team. If you do those two things, it will guide you to make the right decisions that help grow your business."

> Even the greatest of companies do not last forever, but the influence on the people who were nurtured, developed, grown and impacted can leave a lasting legacy that far surpasses sales records and growing profitability.

This story about Patricia, Richard, Dana and Kevin is just one story about one family impacted by the cultural phenomenon of Chick-fil-A. There are likely millions of people who have been impacted by the investments of Chick-fil-A Operators and team members. It is true that treating people with honor, dignity and respect and providing remarkable experiences and unexpected second-mile service strengthens a culture, but even more so, it creates something that is enduring. Even the greatest of companies do not last forever, but the influence on the people who were nurtured, developed, grown and impacted can leave a lasting legacy that far surpasses sales records and growing profitability. It's the stories of the lives that were changed forever that truly define the strength of any culture. Tell a story that matters and steward the story to create a compelling culture that attracts and grows great Talent and delights every guest.

It is my hope that long after the last sandwich is served, the last guest is delighted and the bricks and the mortar crumble, the story of the lives that were impacted will continue. In the end, that is all that really matters. As for me, I am grateful to have been a part of something that truly matters, something bigger than myself and something bigger than a multi-billion dollar company. It's been so worthwhile to play a small part in creating a compelling culture that is not just about a product, but so much more about people.

It is, indeed, my pleasure!

ACKNOWLEDGMENTS

This started out as a blog post that I just kept on writing. It's been cathartic as I mourned the loss, in the same twelve months, of my father, Lee Dailey, who raised me for the first eighteen years and loved me for 31 more, and also the man who guided me in business for all of my adult life, Truett Cathy.

No one ever accomplishes anything worthwhile on their own and I have so many people to whom I am thankful. With deep gratitude, thank you to:

Mark Russell, Anna McHargue, Bobby Kuber and the entire team at Elevate Publishing. You are dedicated to your craft and are an exceptional group of servant-hearted people. Thank you for your patience, guidance and direction throughout this project.

My friends and colleagues: Alli Worthington, Darya Fields, Genia Rogers, Lynn Chastain, Lysa TerKeurst, Pat Booth, Tammy Pearson, Bill Hightower, Kelly Ludwick, Mark Miller, Vickie Garrard, Carrie Kurlander and Lisa Churchfield for your guidance, advice, encouragement and prayers.

Chick-fil-A Operators Tammy Guadagno, Brad Williams, Kevin Williams, K. J. Wari, Rudy Martinez,

Norm Kober, Bruce Ploeser, Margaret Phillips, Joe Dinardo, Jim Larreau, Keith Booth, Becky Pickle, Marla Davis, Sam Poeana, Carmenza Moreno, Shane Todd, Matthew Sexton, Rob Rogers, Mark Meadows, Doug Mickey and former Operators Heather Reddick, Gary Gettis, Tracy Roper, and Shane Benson whose stories fill these pages and whose friendship fills my heart. These leaders have helped make Chick-fil-A a truly remarkable organization.

Truett Cathy, Jimmy Collins, Huie Woods and Brian Ray for hiring me and giving me an opportunity. Dan Cathy and Tim Tassopoulos for growing and developing me all of these years. The influence of all these men transformed my life.

The other culture curators at Chick-fil-A: Bubba Cathy, Perry Ragsdale, Buck McCabe and Steve Robinson. Thank you for mentoring me and offering the gifts of your time and advice.

The Corporate Talent team at Chick-fil-A who make coming to work a joy every single day. They have been partners in the work of attracting, selecting and keeping extraordinary talent.

The thousands of Chick-fil-A staff and Operators for their stories, their love and making imprints on my life. Thank you to millions of Chick-fil-A Raving Fans who support our brand.

Janice Bright, my high school English teacher, who wrote in my yearbok decades ago, "I want an autographed copy of your first book." Every student needs a teacher who fosters a dream.

My dad, Lee Dailey, who is with the Lord and my mother,

Joyce Dailey, who is for me always. I am grateful to have had parents who believe in me.

My children, Trenton, Trevor and Trey, who kept asking, "When are you going to write that book, Mom?" and who are also my "happy thoughts" every single day.

My husband, Ashley, to whom I give the deepest thanks—the man who has loved me and has supported me through every endeavor, joy, heartache, victory and challenge and changed my life when he changed a tire.

And finally, all thanks be to God, who is my everything.

I am among all people, most blessed and most grateful.

ABOUT THE AUTHOR

Dee Ann Turner has worked for Chick-fil-A for more than 30 years and currently serves as Vice President, Corporate Talent. Over the years, she has played an intricate role in growing Chick-fil-A's unique and highly regarded culture while overseeing recruitment, selection, and retention of corporate staff and the recruitment and selection of Chick-fil-A Franchisees.

Dee Ann's insightful knowledge and applicable tools to building an incredible and influential company culture are revealed in her upcoming book, *It's My Pleasure: The Impact of Extraordinary Talent and A Compelling Culture*. Dee Ann attended Cincinnati Christian University in Cincinnati, Ohio, majoring in Journalism and Christian Education. She later completed her education at Clayton State University in Atlanta with a degree in Management. She received further certifications at Goizueta School of Business at Emory University, Darden School of Business at the University of Virginia, Kenan-Flagler Business School at UNC Chapel Hill, and she completed the prestigious Advanced Management Program at Harvard Business School.

Dee Ann serves as a Board member for the Kenya Project, an organization that provides education, homes, food and spiritual growth for children in Kenya. Additionally, she serves as a Board member of Proverbs 31 ministry in Charlotte, N.C. She has a passion for missions that support women and children and strengthen families. Dee Ann and her husband, Ashley, have been married for over 30 years and they have three sons, Trenton, Trevor and Trey.

elevate
publishing

A strategic publisher empowering authors to strengthen their brand.

Visit Elevate Publishing for our latest offerings.

www.elevatepub.com